The Children of Bladensfield

The Children of Bladensfield

by Evelyn D. Ward
with an essay by Peter Matthiessen

A Sand Dune Press Book · The Viking Press · New York

Copyright © Sand Dune Press 1978. All rights reserved. First published in 1978 by The Viking Press, 625 Madison Avenue, New York, N.Y. 10022. Published simultaneously in Canada by Penguin Books Canada Limited. *Printed in the United States of America*

Library of Congress Cataloging in Publication Data
Ward, Evelyn D.
    The Children of Bladensfield.
    "A Sand Dune Press book."
    1.   United   States—History—Civil War, 1861–1865—Personal narratives—Confederate side.   2. Ward, Evelyn D. 3. Virginia—Biography.   4. Bladensfield. Va.   I. Title.
E605.W28   973.8'82'0924   77–21731
ISBN 0–670–21661–5

Front endpaper: *Reproduction of a family letter written during the Civil War, when paper was in short supply.*

Foreword

Bladensfield is one of the very old places in Virginia. One of the two oldest that he knew of, was the surmise of our State Historian and Director of Archaeology when he visited it. Other experts have confirmed his testimony.

There is a pleasant mention of the old place in Lancaster's "Historical Homes and Churches of Virginia."

Naturally, about a spot that has been the home of many individuals, stories of human interest have clustered—stories that illustrate the ideas and manners of their day and also the surge of our humanity, forever moving, yet forever the same.

As the farm was deeded before the present counties of Westmoreland and Richmond were determined upon, the front gate and one of the upper fields are in Westmoreland, the house and the rest of the farm in Richmond County.

According to the Guide Book of the Northern Neck, the house was built about the year 1690, by Nicholas Rochester, of the family of Rochesters who founded the city of Rochester in New York. Tradition says the place was for a time the home of George Eskridge, guardian of Mary Ball, George Washington's mother. We know that it was, during their married lives, the home of Ann Tasker Carter (daughter of Councillor Carter of Nomini Hall) and her husband, John Peck, who succeeded as tutor at Nomini Hall, Philip Vickers Fithian, famous for his diary of his stay in the family of Councillor Carter. Mr. and Mrs. Peck and their daughter Alice lie buried in the "Peck Graveyard" at the foot of the garden at Bladensfield.

In 1842 the place was deeded to the Reverend William Norvell Ward by Harriet Peck (then Mrs. Captain Lucius M. Davis), only surviving daughter of Mr. and Mrs. John Peck. There Mr. Ward and his wife brought up twelve children. The place still continues in the family. The following sketch is a history of the lives of the younger members of this family during the Civil War.

E. D. W.

The Children of Bladensfield During the Civil War

by Evelyn D. Ward

*Written for the great-grandchildren and
the great-great-grandchildren of the old place,
and for all thoughtful people who know
what a mighty help history, heart learned,
is to the present.*

*Evelyn Douglas Ward (the author)
with her grandniece and namesake ("little Evie") at Bladensfield.*

Children, how little you know of the great Civil War. Oh yes, you know the names of the battles, who fought, who won, and the like; but what of the great rush and surge in the hearts of that time? What was right, what was wrong? I want you to know, and history may tell, if it is written. As a contribution, I will tell you the story of the children of your old home during those fateful years. As a child, I saw it. As a child I have to tell it; but it shall be true.

I will begin with one September morning in 1860 when we, the children, came up from the spring with Jack, the fly-brush boy. Every morning, just before breakfast, Jack had to go for a fresh fly-brush and a bucket of fresh water. The woods were lovely at that hour. There was so much to see. Now the fall was coming in, fresh and crisp. Wild hops were in bloom, goldenrod and asters were coming out. Not far from the spring there were two grapevine swings and, if we went early enough, we could get a swing all around, though there were so many of us. There were Stell, Evie, and Fonnie, the little white girls; Amy and Maria, our little black maids, and Lewis, the son of our dear nurse, Louisa. Yet we might manage to get a round before the prayer bell rang, because our grown-up sisters were so often late. Our Father would wait for them, but we were scolded.

This time, just as we were getting around, there went the prayer bell! Out of the swing slid Fonnie, and every one of us went tugging up the hill as fast as we could go. I tell you that Spring Hill is no little tug.

We were in time! There sat your Great-Great-Grandfather with the big leather-backed New Testament open before him. But this morning there were great excitement and talk, and we slid into our places unremarked.

Papa was having prayers in the dining room, not in the hall with the doors open, that marked the passing of summer. Papa began to read. He read such a long psalm that Jack, sitting in the servants' line by the sideboard, went to sleep with his mouth open. I looked at Amy. Amy looked at me. We were very near laughing at prayers.

After prayers the talk began again, and kept up when we were at breakfast. We had heard Mamma and Papa talking on the same subject before. Old Mrs. Grey, who had kept a school in Tappahannock, had died, and some weeks past our Father had been asked to take charge of the school. Now he had decided to accept the offer. No wonder everyone was excited. To go away from Bladensfield where we were born, and had lived all of our lives! It didn't seem possible. Yet Mamma and Papa were quite calmly making plans for the moving.

"Well," said Mamma at last, "one thing I know, we can't sit so long over the breakfast table with all that has to be done waiting for us. Children, you must gather the golden crab apples today."

From that time on, we did seem quite in a bustle. Our Father and our two oldest sisters, Sister Matty and Mamie, were to go to Tappahannock in a few days to get things in order and to prepare for us. We were to follow the first of December.

We children had our jobs, any number of them. There was the sage to be picked for the sausage, the golden crab apples to be gathered for jelly, bags of chinquapins to be gotten in the warm sunshine behind the barn.

After frost came, chestnuts would be dropping freely. We would have to be out early every morning to pick them up before the hogs could get around to the trees and gather them for us. Often while out picking up nuts we would see the great red sun rising in the autumn mist. Dear children, that is a beautiful sight. I would like you to see it, and to have the fun we had filling up our bags. I can see the dear brown nuts now, lying on the fallen leaves around us.

Our biggest job was to pick the cotton, but that would wait till November when the cotton bolls would open. Father always raised a small supply of cotton that was picked by the children of the place, black and white. Aunt Eve spun it; and Mrs. Bartlett, our spry little "po' white" neighbor, living in the Big Woods behind the Porters' farm, wove it into very pretty homespun cloth. Your Great-Grandmother always designed the pattern. I can see her now, wrapping different-colored threads around a board, studying to get the prettiest combination of stripes or checks. She couldn't go to a store and buy different-colored dyes as one can today. She had logwood for black, and used walnut or red-oak bark for brown. She also made blue dye—I don't remember how.

That afternoon we went down to gather the golden crabs. Lucy and Harry led. They were the nearest in age to us, the little girls. Jack, the fly-brush boy, was there too, and all the little fry, white and black. With such a crowd, we couldn't help but have a good time. The orchard was all aglow with the September sun. Lucy and Harry were fine for gathering things. Lucy was nearing thirteen, and Harry eleven. They still played with us at times, and when they came, we knew we should have a good time. There was hardly anything they couldn't do. They and Jack could climb trees like squirrels. To tell the truth, they were to do the main business of apple gathering. We, with the near-baby, little Chan, were there rather as fans, though we could pick up the fallen fruit. Every summer we spent hours and hours paring fruit—peaches, quinces, and apples—to be dried for winter use; now it was put in bags and spread along the windows on the sloping roof to catch the sun. Many a time, before and since, have I seen my dear Mother looking on us with her watchful love, but that time remains in my memory. I rarely see that window through the trees without seeing her again, gazing out.

The dear old home looked so peaceful in the evening sunlight. How awful to leave it for months, even if we were coming back next summer! When Lucy said this, we fell to thinking about Tappahannock. We had never even seen a town, only our little village of Warsaw where we went to church and sometimes to visit friends. It would be exciting to live in a town, for changes rather stirred us.

"I'll tell you what we'll do," said Lucy as we walked back to the house with the apples. "Let's make a whole set of new rag babies, and when we cross the ferry, let's play they are shipwrecked, and throw them into the river."

"Oh!" cried Fonnie in extreme agony. She loved the thought of all those new rag babies, and then to throw them into the river—!

Stell and Evie thought it a fine plan. As soon as they reached the house, they went up into the nursery. It was growing dusk. Lucy got a candle (there were no electric lights, gas, or even kerosene lamps in those days). She put it on a little table near by the chest that held scraps and doll-baby rags, and all of us dived in eagerly to pick out pretty pieces and bits to dress the dolls that were to be sacrificed. What a good time we had! Lucy was delightful. She made such beautiful rag dolls, and was so good to all of us. Harry was lovely, too. He could sew as if he were a girl. He often made things for our dolls.

Of course it would never have occurred to us to throw a "store" doll into the river. We hadn't many of them. They were precious. Our Father and Mother had very little money. Not many of our playthings came to us from a store. Today I could count on my fingers every doll we three little girls possessed. But rag dolls! We had strings—families of them. At Christmastime each one of us made batches of dolls to be put in the stockings of the others.

Now Lucy was busy making beautiful creatures, dressing them gorgeously, and they were all to be thrown into the river! Fonnie handled each one with woe in her face. Especially she loved a boy rag baby dressed in linen trousers, a black Norfolk jacket, and a black-velvet cap. His name was Edwin. Lucy named him that because she said she knew he was a sneak and a tell-tale who wouldn't own up to his bad deeds, and that "Edwin" was a goody-goody name that suited him. The more Edwin was abused, the more Fonnie loved him.

At supper we learned more of the family plans. Children, you can learn a great deal if you will only keep still and listen. Amy, my own dear Amy, was to be left behind to wait on Aunt Eve. Silvie, the cook, and all of her children except Amy were to go. Of course Louisa, our dear nurse, could not be left behind. I was deeply distressed at the thought of being parted from Amy, but things were moving swiftly. There was so much to be done, we had no time to grieve. The next day Louisa took us through Mr. Porter's farm and through the Big Woods to where little Mrs. Bartlett lived. Mrs. Bartlett was to weave the new rag carpet our Mother was making. Louisa went to tell her that we would bring her the warp in a few days, and please not to put anything else in her loom, as Mamma wanted very much to have our carpet finished before December.

*The Reverend William N.
Ward ("Papa").*

"Don't stay," our Mother said to Louisa. "There is so much to be done."

But we couldn't help lingering. The woods were lovely! The air was sweet, and the different branches that we had to cross ran over the stones, talking to themselves and to the minnows and the mellow bugs in such enticing tones. Besides, the chinquapin burrs were opening. With Louisa's help, we filled our pockets as we came. Yet we must have made fairly good time. Mamma didn't scold us when we reached home—warm, tired and happy—hands full of wild hops and goldenrod, pockets bursting with chinquapins.

When we went to bed, Louisa always stayed around till we were asleep. When the moon shone, the long black shadows of the trees moved and twisted across the patch of moonlight on the floor. They looked like arms reaching up to take us. There was something mysterious that we were afraid of. It was called John Brown. We knew that John Brown was dead, but we knew Mamma was still afraid of him, so we were, too. When the shadows twisted, we would call softly, "Louisa!"

Louisa, who might be in Mother's room turning down the beds and watching the baby, would come into the nursery.

Mary B. Ward ("Mamma").

"Now, whut you want? Shut up your eyes, and go to sleep."

"Louisa, is that John Brown climbing up to the window?"

"Don't you be skeered uv John Brown, chile. John Brown is dead and buried."

"Mamma is afraid of him."

"You go on to sleep. Nothin' ain't goin' to hurt you."

But she would sit down by us, and with a hand stretched out to touch her, our fears would vanish into sleep.

———◆∽◆———

The fall days passed, sunny and busy. I don't remember whether we had lessons or not. Our Father and Matty and Mamie were in Tappahannock, where school had begun. Mrs. Bartlett had begun to weave the carpet, but all of the material was not ready. Great-Grandmother had all the family at work on it up in her room. We ran races to see who would sew the largest ball of rags while Mamma tore them, and Louisa and our big sister, Eddie, wound warp. If you should come to Bladensfield, I would show you one of the winding-blades they used. The baby could crawl. He and Chan, who was not much more than a baby, crawled about among us, and got into all kinds of mischief—very troublesome, but so cute! The grownups scolded first, then kissed them.

With November came some dark, rainy weather, chill and raw. Will had finished at the University and was studying law under a good lawyer, Mr. Roy Mason, a friend of my Father's who lived near Fredericksburg. Will tutored in the Mason family while he studied law, but now he had come home to vote, for this November a president was to be elected.

Will had ridden through the rain to Warsaw for the mail. He hoped to hear who was elected. As it began to grow dusk he came in with the news. Lincoln was President! What a stir and buzz of talk! Now there would certainly be war, the grownups were saying. I looked at Mother. She was saying nothing, but looked—I couldn't tell you how she looked. War! And Will would have to go! All the raw chill of the outside came into our pleasant room. I sat by the window watching the cold rain run down the panes. Big drops were running down my cheeks. The dark came, and the work was all put away, but still I sat there, a poor little frozen-hearted thing, seeing misery come to take the place of our happy life.

The grownups went on talking till candles were brought. Presently the supper bell rang out from downstairs. Everybody was going down, but I couldn't move.

I was found crying in the dark. All of them laughed at me. Will said, "The war hasn't come yet. Maybe it never will come. Don't begin to cry beforehand." He took me on his back and carried me down. As we went, I whispered to him that I was crying for fear he would be killed.

In the dining room everything looked bright. There was a fine blaze going up the chimney. The table was ready for us, and Amy was smiling at me from behind my chair. War couldn't come! I wiped my eyes and grew happy again.

At last it was December. Everyone was so busy we didn't have time to worry. I forgot about the war. The new carpet came home and was packed to be made up for the dining room in the Tappahannock house. We took some furniture and bought more from old Mrs. Grey's sale. We couldn't move out

The slave-built baby house.

bag and baggage because we were to spend our summers at Bladensfield. The dolls' house was too big and heavy; besides we couldn't have a whole room for our things in Tappahannock. It was left behind, but we had packed all of our doll things ready to go. The new rag babies that were to be drowned were in a basket to themselves, to go with us on the boat.

We were thrilled with excitement at the thought of all the new experiences waiting for us, but when the last evening came and we collected around the fireplace where our evenings had always been spent, and realized that we were going away, we felt sad and strange. Amy and I felt dreadful at being parted. I took my Mother's scissors and cut a big lock of Amy's short, crisp curls just above her forehead; then she cut a big lock of mine just above my forehead. We said we would always think of each other. The supper bell rang as we finished. Mother dropped her hands when she saw me. "What on earth have you done to yourself?" she exclaimed.

I don't wonder. A large tuft of hair like a man's three-day-old beard stood up above my forehead where smooth, shiny locks had been. Everybody laughed except Mother, who was too disturbed.

"The idea," she said, "of my having to take among strangers a child looking like that!"

I suffered and was ready to cry. It had seemed so natural and right for Amy and me to exchange locks. I hadn't meant any harm. Then someone noticed Amy's head as she stood behind my chair. It was clear what we had done. There was a general laugh again, but this time it was a pleasanter kind of laugh. I was comforted a little, though sorry that I would look like a fright when I went among strangers.

That last morning we had breakfast by candlelight in order to make an early start. I remember it was not very light when we told Aunt Eve and Amy good-bye. Aunt Eve was washing the breakfast china, crying as she washed. My Mother told her she was to come to see us in Tappahannock and bring Amy. We felt sad to be going and to see Aunt Eve crying, but cheered up when we were in the carriage, and the bays, Dick and Pad, were trotting us gaily away.

It was a lovely day, not in the least cold, although it was December. That was fortunate for us, for we had to drive ten miles to the ferry and then cross the Rappahannock in an open horse boat. The river flashed, purple and green and sparkling, and we rejoiced that we were to cross it. Lucy held the basket of rag babies that were to be sacrificed. Ours was certainly a good mother. Crowded in that boat with a baby, all those children, baskets and packages, she let us sit by the edge of the boat and throw our rag dolls overboard, one by one, and wail and lament to watch them drown. Poor little Fonnie! It was no play to her. She looked sadly on, almost in tears when her beloved Edwin and a little girl with long golden curls of worsted, wearing a black-velvet skirt and pink bodice, went floating off.

What a shiny place we found Tappahannock to be when we finally beached at the foot of Main Street. I have seen many a town since, in America and in Europe, but none ever wore such a shiny smile for me. Father, Sister Matty and Mamie were there to meet us. My! They laughed and talked as we went in a long procession up Main Street. Friends came out to their doors to wave a welcome and call to us as we went. To us, little backwoods people, it was very interesting to be living so intimately with others.

Mamma said the Old Grey House was the most inconvenient house she had ever seen, but we were delighted with it. There were so many surprises. When you went from the dining room into an inner passageway

One of the first kerosene lamps—1860.

and walked a few steps, you had to take a step down. Then, when you went a little farther, you had to step up again. Our Mother said it was going to cause us many a fall, but we liked it. We liked our Mother's room at the end of the passage to the west, and the long, brick-floored, covered way, sunny and bright, just a step away. We knew that was where we should play in bad weather. It led to the schoolhouse where Father and Sister Matty and Mamie were teaching the Tappahannock children—a day school. There were no public schools in Virginia then.

When we went out to explore the lot, we found a dear old garden with flowerbeds and long walks everywhere. One of the walks went entirely through the lot, and at the end was a gate under a big wild cherry tree. On Sundays we used to walk that way to church. At Bladensfield we had to hustle up and drive five miles to church. Some of us always had to be left at home—not that we minded much; it was fun at home.

As we finished exploring the grounds, twilight began to fall. We came back to the house, thinking of supper, and bumped up against a porch we had not seen before. A little boy was standing on it. Thinking to have gone by mistake into one of the many yards belonging to our new neighbors, we felt badly, and wondered what we should do, but the little boy called to us, and looking more closely at him, we discovered it was our own little three-year-old, Chan. This was only another proof of the rambling nature of our new home, for the porch belonged to the Grey House. It was a pleasant, square enclosure, just outside the pantry. Quite a flight of steps led to the ground and another flight went down into the cellar.

Coming into the dining room, we were met by the biggest surprise of all. We had never seen any lights but candles. A few candles for ordinary times, a great many for special occasions. Now in the middle of the table was a kerosene lamp, giving—oh! so much light! I mention this especially because kerosene lamps were then a new invention. Bourne's *School History of the United States* says, "Kerosene lamps were invented during the Civil War." My Father always kept an eye open for any new invention. In remote little Tappahannock in 1860 he had procured two kerosene lamps—one for the parlor and one for the dining room. The parlor lamp we still use. It has a glass bowl and a brass stem.

In the morning of our first day in school (we had always had lessons at home), we gathered our books and went solemnly down the long covered way to the schoolhouse. Even little Fonnie had her *McGuffey's First Reader*, though she was only five years old. It hardly seemed possible it could be our Sister Matty presiding over the big girls—some looked like grownups! We took our books to the other end of the big room where our Sister Eddie, with her hair tucked up, was teaching the little children. A little we studied, and a good deal we looked around at the other children, who were hard at work looking at us.

At recess we got quite a little acquainted. There was Betty Brockenbrough, about Stell's age, who was to be our special friend, Sister Matty said; Brockenbrough Blake, a big, kind-looking, red-headed boy, behind in his lessons, and in with the little ones. He was always good-natured and kind to us. We were devoted to him. There were Selden and Joney Wright, and tiny little Sperry Wilmo Hearn, no bigger than a match, but bright and quick to learn. He was the son of the man who had a little repair shop not far from the Old Church.

The older pupils thought themselves too grown up to play at recess, but the rest of us were only too glad when the bell rang. We played Hi Spy every day, big and little ones, and never seemed to tire of it. The Old Grey House garden had such lovely places for hiding, and such splendid runways. We soon felt very much at home in Tappahannock.

Our dog, Crab, must have missed us sadly. He was shut up when we left Bladensfield, but two days later he was standing by the front door, panting and wagging his tail. We were delighted to see him and wondered how on earth he had found out where we were; but Father said his place was at Bladensfield, and sent him home. The overseer chained him to a heavy block, but several days afterward he came again, dragging the block with him. A fisherman came with him and told my Father he had seen Crab struggling in the water, about to drown. The fisherman said he picked up the block and watched to see in what direction Crab would go. The dog swam manfully across the river. As the fisherman was crossing to Tappahannock also, he put the block in the boat and let Crab follow him. Dear old Crab was sent home again. I don't remember that he came a third time.

As our house was directly in front of the Court House we saw a great many things going on. One Monday in each month was Court Day, and such a crowd of people always came! The farmers from far and near drove in with their queer vehicles and tied their horses to our side paling. That was decidedly bad for the paling. The horses chewed and gnawed it and sometimes pawed and kicked it; but that seemed to be the custom, so your Great-Grandfather made no complaint. We children soon got great profit from it. There was, just then, a vogue among the little pupils of the school for rings woven of horsehair. It was difficult for most of the children to procure horsehair, but not for us. As soon as the farmers had tied their horses and were gone about their business, we went around making a collection from black tails, sorrel tails, and white tails. We would thrust our hands through the paling, catch a few strands of horse's tail, and give a yank. Often the horse gave furious kicks. It was a wonder we were not killed, but we weren't, and we hardly ever failed to bring away the hair.

The first Court Day after we came to Tappahannock, we saw a sight that I am thankful, children, you will never see. Among the crowds in front of the Court House were groups of colored people: men, women, boys, and girls, each with a little bundle or bag, and before them a white auctioneer calling out in his loud voice. He was hiring them out and sometimes selling them. Most of this occurred at the January Court, but there were a few instances at other Court Days. Often we used to watch this sad sight from the window of Mother's happy, comfortable room, and I am glad she bade us see how sad it was.

Yet at this January Court a delightful experience came to us from this same sad occurrence. While we were watching through the window, Father came into the room followed by a strange colored girl fourteen or fifteen years old. We had seen her standing by the auctioneer, a bright-eyed, brown-faced slip of a girl with a bundle tied up in a big bandanna handkerchief. Our Father had hired her for the winter to help Louisa with the baby and to look after us. Her name was Clara (pronounced Claira). She belonged to a distant relation of ours who lived some miles out of Tappahannock.

We were friends with Claira as soon as we looked at each other. Many a pleasant hour we had with her, and I think she was happy with us. We would gladly do as much of her work as we could to get her off to play. She taught us to weave the dearly prized horsehair rings, was fine about dressing little dolls and making rag babies, and had the most beautiful stories to tell about her own home, and Miss Josie, her little mistress. Josie Lewis's father, our cousin, was dead, and Josie and her mother lived alone on their big plantation. Mrs. Lewis was quite wealthy. She had a great many "people," and Claira loved to tell us of little Josie's playthings and possessions. Through Claira's stories, Josie grew to be quite a romance with us. With Hi Spy with the school children in the garden during the day, and games with ourselves and Claira in the evenings, we had a good time that winter.

I don't think Mother enjoyed the winter very much. Water rose continually in the cellar. Children are such unthinking creatures, we didn't worry over the menace of that, being more interested in the process of bailing out the water. Chan had pneumonia, and was very ill. Then Fonnie had

Left to right: Estelle, Lucy, and Evelyn Ward (Stell, Lucy, and Evie).

diphtheria, a new disease in 1861. The doctor said he didn't know how to treat it, and that no one knew. Poor little Fonnie was very ill. I don't think she would have lived if she hadn't been nursed by our good Mother. Her legs and throat were paralyzed, she could neither walk nor swallow; but Mamma and Dr. Gordon managed to feed her, and Mamma would hold her up so that her feet just reached the floor, and would move her back and forth; and after a while she could walk and swallow, laugh and play. Chan got well too. We were distressed to see Fonnie and Chan so ill, and were anxious about them, yet I remember enjoying much about that winter.

Brother Will came to spend some days with us, and made everybody glad from Mother down to Baby Ran. Brother Will was the best brother that ever lived. There was always company in the parlor, and Sister Matty, Mamie, and Eddie were much taken up with it after school hours. Always Tom or Lal Roane, or our new cousins, Waring and Philip Lewis, or some of the Latanes, or a host of others were there, and the girls had to entertain them; but Brother Will stayed with Mamma and Lucy and us. One day he roasted oysters for us in the dining room, feeding us all around, picnic style, as fast as he could roast them.

When she was out of school, Lucy was always helping Mamma in the housekeeping or sewing for us. I remember her little workbasket, always piled full of socks and stockings to be darned. Nobody told her to do it. She thought of things herself. She must have been the best child of thirteen that ever lived. She was grand for playing, too, and beat everybody at Hi Spy or Blind Man's Buff. We knew we should have a fine time when she left her work and came to lead our plays.

One day late in the winter when Fonnie and Chan were well again, Louisa took us for a long walk over the Long Bridge. We had a tip-top time. Coming back in the twilight, we met at our gate a sway-backed little old colored woman dressed in a warm linsey dress and cloak and hood. A little colored girl was with her. We looked at her a minute before we saw it was Aunt Eve and Amy. My! How glad we were, and when we took them in, Mamma was as glad as we. They stayed a week. Mamma took care of Aunt Eve and we kept Amy with us, and showed her the sights of Tappa-hannock.

All the time there was war talk going on. I had grown used to it and did not cry over it any more. In those days there was a regular militia force maintained and drilled in Virginia, and we loved to see General Upshur, dressed in his blue uniform with brass buttons and wearing a great floating-top plume in his hat, lead out his soldiers and drill them on Main Street. Then Captain Walter Jones would come with his cavalry. My! How grand he looked with his plume, his buttons, his epaulets and sash, and his long sword. If you go to the secretary at Bladensfield, you may see a picture of him with his sword half drawn—very fierce for a militiaman. It is a daguerreotype that he gave Sister Matty. As the winter drew toward spring there was more and more drilling, and more and more war talk. I know now what was happening. I don't know that I understood it then.

I did know when Mr. Lincoln called for troops from all the states, and when Fort Sumter fell. How excited everyone was! It didn't seem to me that anyone was sorry about it except Mamma. She could not bear to speak of it. However, life and lessons went on as usual. Spring was coming on, warm and bright. One evening in April was so warm our Mother let us take off our shoes and stockings and dance under the plum tree that was near the covered way.

A few days later, two men in a fishing smack were taken prisoner and lodged in the Tappahannock jail. We heard they were "Yankee spies." After we had gone to bed the evening before, someone had brought the news that a Yankee cruiser, the *Pawnee*, was at the mouth of the Rappahannock River and was on her way to Tappahannock. It seemed exciting to us children, but we played, had our lessons, and slept soundly. Then, in the middle of the night, our Mother, with a drawn, white face, leaned over us and told us to get up and dress quickly, "The Yankees have come." We found candles lighted in all of the rooms and everyone moving. Louisa was dressing the baby and Mamma was putting some of our clothes into the carpetbag.

While eating a hurried breakfast by candlelight, I heard the grownups say the Yankee spies were standing in the street before our house, under guard of the Tappahannock militia. Mr. Lal Roane came in and said their hearts were beating so hard one could almost hear them, and that they thought they were about to be shot. Of course they were not. They were only taken to Richmond.

Our cousin, old Mr. Warner Lewis, had sent his carriage to take us to his home in the country; his daughter-in-law, Josie Lewis's mother, had sent hers also, and everything was ready for us to start. In the gray light outside, Cousin Warner Lewis's carriage was drawn up, with old Uncle Bailor holding the horses, and Mrs. Lewis's carriage behind it. Father was to stay to help defend Tappahannock, and keep the *Pawnee* from passing farther up the river. Mamie was to stay too, for a while, and the servants, except Louisa. Claira was to visit her own home while we should be away. Our brother Charley was at Bladensfield overseeing the overseer. Still, there were a good many to go, since Father insisted that Mamma must take the children away from any danger. There were Sister Matty, Eddie, Lucy, and Harry besides the little children and the baby. I don't remember why all of us except Stell went to Lewis Level, Cousin Warner Lewis's place, when Josie's mother had been so kind as to send her carriage to take us to her house, but we did. We thought Stell very brave to go all by herself to stay with Mrs. Lewis. She thought she would enjoy playing with Josie whom Claira had talked about so much.

It was a lovely April morning. I remember how pretty the country looked, and we were glad to get out into it again, away from Tappahannock. Although we were considerably bunched up in the carriage, we enjoyed the drive. Lewis Level was a dear old place. Cousin Warner Lewis named it Lewis Level because he said so many people named their places Mount Aery when there wasn't any mount, or Oak Grove when there weren't any oaks; he named his plain Lewis Level because that was what it was. It was a long, rather low-pitched brick house that spread out and seemed to run around over quite a space of ground, with entrances and odd little porches where you least expected them. Cousin Warner, his wife, Cousin Sarah; their daughter, sweet Cousin Kitty Rouzie, with her two children; and Cousin Robert Lewis came out to receive us. Cousin Sarah, I remember, cried as she kissed us, because we had had "to run away from the Yankees."

"Poor little ones," she said, "didn't you even have time to dress your dollies?" For our dolls' dresses were still unfastened.

Then she turned to her son, Cousin Robert, and began to talk to him with her hands. He was a mute. We had never seen him before and didn't know he couldn't hear. It looked as though Cousin Sarah had suddenly lost her senses. She puffed out her cheeks and blew to show how the Yankees would shoot, then she straddled a finger of her left hand with two of her right to show how we were riding away from them, and used a great many other very vivacious signs. Cousin Robert nodded his head comprehendingly and patted our shoulders to show his sympathy.

The Lewises made us welcome and were as good as gold to us all the time we stayed at their house. Lewis Level was a new experience for us. At Bladensfield we had "people" enough to supply house servants and farm hands, and Aunt Eve to spin the wool and cotton necessary to make home-spun clothes for all the colored people; but at Lewis Level there were troops of colored people, all well clothed and contented looking, and a good many different kinds of manufacture were carried on. Leather was tanned there, and in one house was a shoemaker who made shoes for not only all the colored people, but also made really dainty-looking calfskin shoes for the ladies of the family. Then there were spinners, several of them. One room in the basement was the weaving room. The weaver, however, was not a Negro but a "po' white"—"Cousin Milly," the children at Lewis

Level called her—a kind-faced, gentle-mannered woman somewhere in her thirties. Our Mother told us she had been left without a home and the Lewises had taken her to live at Lewis Level. She helped Mrs. Lewis with the housekeeping and did the weaving. She was very good to us while we were there.

After we had had dinner and had rested awhile, Mrs. Lewis called a bright-looking yellow girl, who might have been eighteen or nineteen, and told her to show us about the place. Mrs. Lewis told her she must take care of us while we were at Lewis Level and help us to enjoy ourselves. Her regular work was knitting socks and stockings. She carried her knitting in a big pocket of her apron and whenever she stopped, she would take it out and knit very rapidly. She took us to see the shoemaker, busily making shoes. We sat down and talked to him a good while and then went to see the spinners.

It must have been a puzzle for Cousin Sarah Lewis to put away such a family as ours, added to her own already large one. Then we learned that the wagon that was bringing our trunks and bags had not arrived. What were we to do for night clothes? Fonnie was little, she could wear one of little Kitty Rouzie's nightgowns, but what was I to wear? Cousin Sarah brought out one of Catesby's shirts. Catesby was her son, about the age of our Harry. The shirt was big enough for two of me, but wrapped in it, and lying on that soft pallet, I went so fast asleep that I never knew one thing till I was wakened by the sun shining through the window and Louisa standing over us, ready to help us dress.

Everything was delightfully new and strange around us. We had the freedom of the place, though, of course, we had been trained where to go and where not to go in the house of our hostess. We had sweet Cousin Kitty Rouzie's little Kitty and her little brother to go with us; and Catesby and Harry played with us though they were several years older than we. We often thought about Stell and wondered what she and Josie were doing, and if she were having as good a time as we.

We must have gone to Lewis Level about Easter, for Catesby was not at school, and a day or two after we arrived two other members of the Lewis family came for a holiday from their school in Staunton. One was a sweet, lovely girl of sixteen, Lucy Temple Lewis; the other a boy, Fielding, younger than Catebsy. Both of those were deaf, and consequently mute, as teaching the deaf had progressed very little in 1861. They were taught a sign language in Staunton, as well as reading, writing, and the ordinary studies, but no one, I think, had up to that time undertaken to teach speech to a person deaf from babyhood. It was very interesting to me then and very touching as I recall the gentleness and consideration of all the other Lewises toward the three afflicted with deafness. Lucy Temple was really beautiful, and very gentle and attractive with her graceful sign language and her pretty ways. Fielding was handsome. He had great, flashing dark eyes. I think he must have been more than usually intelligent, and was very passionate. I suppose that came from his difficulty in expressing himself. His mother tried to teach him to speak. He could say "apple pie" distinctly. When he was pleased and happy, he would look around smiling, and say, "Apple pie, apple pie." He could say "Foo," trying to say "fool." I don't know how he learned that, but when he was angry, his great eyes would flash and he would call out, "Foo, foo!"

Before he came, we had followed little Kitty Rouzie into the housekeeper's room in the evening to grind the coffee for supper. There was a big grinder like ours at Bladensfield, with a great iron wheel. We took turns grinding. The evening after Fielding came, we were grinding away when he came in. He ran up, took little Kitty by the chin, and boxed her severely, crying, "Foo! Foo!"

"He always grinds the coffee when he is here," said dear little Kitty in self-reproach as she rubbed her tingling cheeks. "I should have remembered." Ordinarily, however, he was very pleasant and played with us merrily.

The days were growing warmer and lovelier. We spent most of our time in the woods. Catesby and Harry made for themselves, and for us, chestnut whistles that made sweet, flutelike notes, though each would be on a different key. There are no chestnut trees now. Sometimes these whistles made sharp, treble sounds; sometimes, big, bullfrog blows, and sometimes really sweet sounds, like bugles. One day we came up through the garden walk, all blowing for dear life, no matter what kind of sound each whistle made. Poor old Cousin Warner was on the porch. He put his hands to his ears and called out, "My God, Sarah, drive them out, drive them out!"

After we had been at Lewis Level two or three days, our brother Will came unexpectedly. He had been to Tappahannock, and there learned where we were. He told us the *Pawnee* had never started to come up the river, and the "Yankee spies" sent to Richmond were only some fishermen or traders who had wanted to do a little business with the Tappahannock people. We had had all of our scare for nothing. Brother Will was to go back that evening, and the rest of us would follow in the morning. He proposed to take me back in the buggy with him; but Mamma said I was so sleepy-headed when night came that she was afraid I would go to sleep and fall out of the buggy. She said Fonnie might go because she could keep awake. I knew it was true. I was sleepy-headed and Fonnie always bright-eyed and wide awake; but oh, what a terrible slam that was to me! And how dreadfully I felt when I watched Fonnie drive off with Brother Will! It was such an honor for him to choose me, and so dreadful to be sleepy-headed!

It was Sunday evening when they went. Mrs. Lewis's (Josie's mother's) plantation was not far from Lewis Level. Claira came that evening to go back with us. While we watched the buggy drive away we saw Claira coming back over the field, and what do you think! Stell was with her! Poor Stell, carrying a little bag of clothes, had run away! She had been so homesick, and when Claira started to leave, she couldn't stand it any longer. She crept upstairs, put her things in her bag, and sneaked off with her without even a word of good-bye to Mrs. Lewis or Josie.

Stell was near crying, but she didn't. We were glad to get her back. It was a pity for her to have been so lonely and homesick while we were having a good time; but she was with us now, and we were going home in the morning. Stell said Mrs. Lewis and Josie were as good to her as could be, she was just homesick. I suppose Mamma made it all right with Mrs. Lewis.

We went back to Tappahannock on the twenty-ninth of April, Fonnie's birthday. She had torn her best dress, and was feeling very badly about it when we arrived. We had very little money and had to take care of our best things.

"Don't scold her, Mamma," Brother Will said. "She had no other dress to wear till you brought her some, and she couldn't help tearing it."

There was one thing our Mother never could resist—that was doing whatever Brother Will wanted. She never said a word about the torn dress—just gave Fonnie another to wear—and Lucy took the best dress and mended it so neatly it was as good as ever. We were very glad to get home. The snowballs were in bloom, for that was an early spring. There were a great many snowball bushes in the old Grey House garden, and lilacs, and in the borders were banks of heart's-ease, violets, and other dear little flowers.

In Tappahannock, there was drilling in the streets now everyday. Mr. Lal Roane, Mr. Austen Brockenbrough, and the Latanes were drilling men without any uniforms. The oddest thing was that these young men would come into Father's study and he would drill them. He would have our older sisters in too, with brooms and the pokers held for guns just as we did when we played soldier, and would march them up and down the room. Father was educated at West Point, but later determined to be a clergyman instead of a soldier. He knew all the drills and movements of soldiers, and was teaching the young men that they might drill their men correctly. Each of these young men was trying to organize a company for the regiment that was to be the Fifty-fifth Virginia. The War had actually begun! I didn't feel afraid now. It was very interesting to watch the drilling in the study and then the drilling in the streets, both cavalry and infantry, and we learned the drills, too. We could shoulder arms, carry arms, right-about face, guide right, and guide left, right wheel, left wheel, march, double-quick, and often did it instead of playing Hi Spy in the old garden. We learned to keep step beautifully.

Essex County was organizing the Fifty-fifth for the War, and Cousin Waring Lewis, Mr. Tom Roane, and some of the other young men were getting up the Essex Troop, a cavalry company. Their horses were rubbed up very shiny, their manes and tails waved, and their nostrils seemed to snort red fire. Beautiful but awful-looking creatures they seemed to us, yet their riders seemed as much at home on their backs as if they were walking on the ground. Especially we loved to watch Mr. Tom Roane on his big black horse. He could do so many things on horseback. He would come sweeping up the street at full gallop, throw down his hat, whirl under his horse's stomach, pick up the hat, and ride off without slacking speed.

Cousin Waring was captain of the Essex Troop, which was sworn in at the Court House. We watched them go in, and our Mother, on the lookout, saw Charley go in with them. She sent for Cousin Waring and told him that Charley was only sixteen and she positively forbade his going into the army. My poor Mother! Brother Will had already joined the Forty-seventh Regiment, gotten up in Westmoreland County. She could not stand to have Charley go too, so Cousin Waring spoke to him and sent him out to her. Charley wanted to go with the others, but he gave in to his Mother without ill temper. She promised that if the War continued till he was eighteen—the draft age—she would not say a word against his going. Then she sent him back to Bladensfield to oversee the overseer.

Cousin Philip Lewis went into his brother Waring's troop as a private. He was just eighteen. Old Cousin Warner had planned to send him to the University. Cousin Warner was a good father but an autocrat in his household. Most of his children were afraid to say their souls were their own if he opposed them. Not so Philip, his best beloved, who was to go to the University. Mr. Lewis told his son this with his usual finality, but Philip looked at him with his gentle eyes, and said steadily, "Father, you know I am eighteen. I am going into the army."

His father fumed and blustered. He "would hear none of such nonsense." He bade his wife get "the Boy's" clothes ready. Philip said nothing more.

Finally the day and hour for going arrived. Mrs. Lewis had packed her son's bag.

"Come, my son," old Mr. Lewis said when Uncle Bailor drove the carriage up. "Everything is ready. It is time for you to go."

Philip was reading. He looked up and said in his quiet voice, "But, Father, you know I am not going. I am going to join the army."

Poor old man! He knew "the Boy" was right. He threw his arms around him, laid his head on that brave young breast, and wept his heart out. Philip held him and comforted him as best he could.

The Fifty-fifth Virginia still lacked its quota of companies. Mr. Lal Roane and Mr. Austen Brockenbrough went into the country and routed out a hundred of the oddest-looking men that anyone ever saw. They didn't seem able to stand up straight and they didn't know their right foot from their left. The young officers named them the Jefferson Davis Rifles, and drilled them diligently on the back street. We used to lie on top of the althea hedge in our garden to watch the drills. One day we each caught a bumblebee in an althea bloom and, creeping cautiously to the paling, threw the bumblebee right into the midst of the Jefferson Davis Rifles. The country boys all scattered, some laughing, some saying bad words at us. The poor hot, tired young officers were disgusted. Mr. Austen Brockenbrough corralled us in a corner of the paling and gave us a good scolding. He told us if ever we did anything like that again he would take us to our Mother and see that we got the whipping we deserved.

After hard drilling, the Jefferson Davis Rifles learned to put out the

The chair in which Reverend William N. Ward wrote his sermons.

right foot or the left when it was called for, to straighten themselves up, and they began to look quite like soldiers. Once Mr. Lal Roane marched his squad directly across the street to our gate. There was a sidewalk with a curb there. Before the soldiers quite reached the curb, they stopped without any command from their officer. I never shall forget Mr. Lal's odd manner of taking this move. He came up in front of the line and stood looking at his men. Then he said in his soft, slow drawl, "*Soldiers* never stop till they are ordered to stop. If I march you up to the Major's house, and don't order you to halt, you are to get through the windows and doors, or hop over the house, but you are never to halt till you are ordered to do so."

He never raised his voice, but the men looked utterly crushed. I have always wondered how Mr. Lal with such a soft voice managed to make his men feel so badly.

One very bright, sunny day we were down on the river shore with Claira. As we lay there basking in the sunshine, we saw three boats crossing, loaded with men. The men wore dark-blue uniforms and carried rifles, and after they landed, they stood in squads in the shade of the old Parker House trees while three of their leaders went up Main Street. Very soon they came back with Father among them. Then began great doings—counting and inspecting, I suppose. We had to go home. Father didn't come home for dinner or for supper either. After we had eaten our supper, a queer-looking little fellow dressed in a blue uniform came to the door, saying the Major had sent him, and that he was to tell Mrs. Ward to give him the Major's dinner.

"Are you to take the Major's dinner to him?" my Mother asked.

"No, Ma'am," said the little fellow, grinning, "I am to eat it for him."

Then he told her that he belonged to the Westmoreland Blues who had come over to join the Fifty-fifth; that none of them as yet had had anything to eat, and the Major was busy providing quarters for them.

"What are you doing with the Westmoreland Blues?" my Mother asked.

"I'm one of 'em, Ma'am," he answered proudly.

"What! You! You are nothing but a child."

"I'm fo'teen, Ma'am."

"You? Fourteen?" answered my Mother. "You don't look it."

"Yes," he said regretfully, "I'm little, but I am tall enough to stick a Yankee in his breadbasket."

"Oh!" cried Mamma, "you horrid little creature!"

The boy grinned as though to say, "Yes, you are a woman, and that is the way you should feel. But I am a man."

Mamma gave him his dinner, and we stood around watching him eat it. He had a man's appetite at least, and a perfect sang-froid. When he had finished, he went back to his company.

The next morning, two or three squads had taken possession of the shade of our trees—of those that grew close to the paling on the side street between our lot and Mrs. Roy's. The boys climbed the paling to watch the cooking operations. We little girls knew we mustn't go so near, but we stood on the platform of the well, trying to see. Who do you think was doing the cooking? The same little fellow who was tall enough to stick a Yankee in his breadbasket!

Eddie came out to watch the soldiers with us. She was greatly interested when she saw who was cooking. "You don't know how to cook," she said to him over the paling.

"Yes, I does, Ma'am."

"See, you are going to mix those biscuits just with water. They won't be fit to eat."

"Well, Ma'am, I ain't got nothin else to mix 'em with. You bet them ez 'as got to eat 'em can do it."

"You come here into our kitchen," said our sister, "and our cook will give you some milk and lard. That will make your bread better."

The boy waited for no second invitation. He opened the gate and promptly brought his big tray of flour into our kitchen. We all pressed up close to watch him pound his big lump of dough.

"Tell us what your name is," said my sister.

"Anton, Ma'am, is my name."

"Well, Anton, I don't think your father should have let you join the army. You are too young."

Anton was pinching his bread off in lumps now, to make hoe-cakes. "I ain't got no father, Ma'am," he said.

"Then your mother."

"I ain't got no mother."

"Your guardian shouldn't have let you come."

Anton peered around sideways at my sister. "I ain't got no guardian," he said with a derisive laugh, "nor a Gordly cent to guard."

"Poor Boy!" my sister said softly.

Anton picked up his tray to be off. "Don't be pitying me," he said impatiently, "I ain't used to nothin. Pity them ez 'as got sweethearts and things."

After that we saw a good deal of Anton. Often when he was passing, our Mother would send us out with something for him—a cake or a roll, or maybe an apple—and he was always gracious and receptive.

Another member of the Westmoreland Blues who attracted our notice was Mr. Childs, a bluff, red-faced fellow of thirty or forty years. Generally he had been drinking. Evidently he had noticed Anton's success with us and would have liked to secure some of this petting. He would stand for long times at the corner of our lot, swaying a little as if too drunk to stand firmly, beckoning over the paling. It didn't seem to matter whether or not anyone was in sight. Eddie enjoyed him. She would let him beckon and call softly, "Oh! Ma'am," for some time, then she would go out and ask:

"What do you want, Mr. Childs?"

Mr. Childs always answered, "Ain't had a mufful t'eat sence Gord A'mighty made me!"

"Why, Mr. Childs," my sister would say, "You are very fat."

"Don' ker 'f I is, I ain't had a mufful t'eat sence Gord A'mighty made me."

Sometimes he got something, for he was a harmless soul, and a soldier; sometimes not. He was so big and red faced.

The Regiment was organizing. President Jefferson Davis sent down a commission for our Father as chief officer. The President wanted to commission him a colonel, but your Great-Grandfather said besides being a clergyman, he was too old for active soldiering, though he could organize the Regiment. He asked for the commission of major, and said he would be ready to deliver the Regiment to its regular officers as soon as it was properly drilled.

There was regimental drill now every morning and dress parade in the evening. All of Tappahannock dressed up in its best to see the dress parade. We thought Father looked splendid, dressed in his dark-blue clothes (the Virginia uniform) with a rather high hat. He stood before the line very tall and straight. A mulatto with a flute and a little drummer boy who beat his drum quite well made very good marching music. We sometimes saw the mulatto in our kitchen talking to Louisa. It was she who tied the pink ribbon on the flute of the "flauter," as she called him. We noted the pink ribbon as the flauter passed up and down the line. We loved to see the Officer of the Day (or whatever he was called—he was plain Mr. Baker when he wasn't drilling) come up, put his hand on his heart, and tell how many soldiers were absent.

A great many new drills were taught. The one that interested us the most was fire-and-load-lying. That is how I remember the order, though it sounds more sensible to say, "Load-and-fire-lying." The men loaded their guns as they lay stretched out on their backs, rolled over, shot, then stretched out and loaded again. One day there was another new drill. The

A desk in the schoolroom at Bladensfield.

men were ordered to lay their guns out on the ground before them. There seemed to be some hesitation about following the order: we perched on the top of the paling, wondering. The men stood holding their guns and whispered together, up and down the line. Father repeated the order, and the under-officers gave it to each company, but there was no response from the men. Then two men were sent forward to speak for them. They saluted and told Father they would never learn that drill. It was the form followed in surrender. Father looked at the men, as if he did not know exactly what to do. Then he turned to the Regiment. To us his face looked strangely moved. He gave the order, "Shoulder arms," and marched it back to barracks.

The Fifty-fifth never learned that drill, and it never needed it. Quite late in the War, when the grownups were reading aloud accounts of a great battle—I don't remember which battle it was—they read that as the battle hung in the balance and a force of Federal troops had to be driven back, the order to charge was given. A regiment of the Gray's went sweeping forward. They drove back the Federals, but were themselves killed down to a handful. General Lee on Traveler, watching the battle, asked:

"What regiment was that?"

"The Fifty-fifth Virginia," was the answer.

"Three cheers for the Fifty-fifth Virginia!" he called.

They gave it—all the soldiers who had seen the gallant action, and the handful of men returning. In the midst of the battle the cheers burst out from line to line as the Grays pressed on. It was a funeral song. There was no more Fifty-fifth. The next morning, the handful left was thrown into another regiment.

As spring advanced, a great number of strangers came to Tappahannock. Very often they were army and naval officers who had resigned to come South. After their resignation they were subject to arrest, and had to get through Maryland and across the Potomac secretly as best they could. Once across, the safest way to Richmond was over the ferry to Tappahannock where all strangers reported to our Father. Our parlor was generally thronged with visitors. We were allowed to come into the parlor if we were very quiet. There were two little mahogany stools with embroidered covers that stood one at each end of the long sofa. We two little girls sat on them. Stell was so old and knew so well what to do that she went among the company as she liked. Colonel Custis Lee was one of those that came; and Zarvona Thomas. General Pickett stayed in Tappahannock several weeks. I remember listening to him when he told that in the Mexican War at one time a mine was dug under a city to defeat a siege. He, then a slim young lieutenant, was the first man squeezed through. He found himself in a room full of Mexican ladies. They all ran to him, screaming, and threw their arms around his knees, his neck, anywhere they could reach, begging for protection.

One day after we had gone to bed, a young man came from Baltimore who had been paralyzed when a child. One leg was shorter than the other. He wore a shoe with a high heel and a very heavy sole. By that means, and with a cane, he walked pretty well. This gentleman spent the night at our house. In the morning, before breakfast, our Mother told us about him. She made Jack, the shoe boy, bring in this shoe for us to see and look at as much as we liked, because, she said, none of us by any means must look at it when our guest was wearing it, as that might hurt his feelings. We went into breakfast with our heads all turned carefully away even when we spoke to Mr. Latrobe, but he said gaily, "See here, I have something to show you," and he threw his short leg over the other one and showed us his tiny foot with its high heel and thick sole. He was so gay and sweet and talked to us so kindly, we liked him more than we did most of the strangers who had two good legs. He looked like a Frenchman. He was of a French family, had black hair and eyes, and a gay, pleasant manner.

Once a thin, withered old lady came, a Mrs. Alexander from Baltimore. Her son had tried to come South but had been taken prisoner, and was held in Fort McHenry. I am not sure, but I think he must have been among those Baltimoreans who fought the troops that were marched through Baltimore on their way South, for there was talk of his being hanged because he had fought and killed when he did not belong to the Southern army. His mother was on her way to Richmond to get a commission for her son from President Davis. Mrs. Alexander went to Richmond, and the son obtained the commission of colonel. Now she had to get the commission through the Northern lines to her son in prison. She ripped the lining of her bonnet (ladies then wore bonnets that closed around the face something like a cap), and put the commission inside. I remember hearing her say to Mamma as she sewed back the lining, "If they feel the paper in there, I shall tell them that ladies often put paper in the crowns of their bonnets to protect them from the oil of the hair."

She started off, brave little old lady, and took the commission to her son. For some time we heard nothing more from her. Then a man came to Tappahannock—Oh! Such a black-haired man! His eyes were the brightest black eyes I ever saw, his big mustache was black, parted over very red lips. His teeth were white and shining. He looked just like a pirate to us. It was Colonel Alexander. He had jumped from the parapet of Fort McHenry and broken the main bone in his leg by the force of his fall into the water. With his leg broken, he swam to shore, crawled into hiding till nightfall, then crawled to some little nearby house. Fortunately the people of the house were friendly to him. They took him covered up in hay in a wagon as far south as they could, and left him at the house of another farmer who would help him. In that way he was taken to Leonardtown, crossed in a fishing smack, and was then brought to the Tappahannock ferry and over to our house. He stayed at our house while he was in Tappahannock. We didn't exactly like him, but he interested us. One day at breakfast while he was talking very eagerly, he gesticulated with his knife, mapping out something on the table with it. Mamma couldn't stand that.

"Man!" she cried, "Don't you scratch my table!"

She was proud of our dining table. It is very fine mahogany, and was old even then. Colonel Alexander smiled till his big black mustache parted and showed his red lips and shining white teeth. He didn't care in the least. "Mother is facetious this morning," he said, but he put the knife down.

There was a Captain Baldwin who had resigned from the United States Navy. Everyone liked him. He was a pleasant, dignified man. While he was at our house, our grown sisters and some other Tappahannock girls were making a flag for the Fifty-fifth Virginia out of a United States flag. Captain Baldwin sat by as, laughing and chatting, the girls ripped the old flag to pieces. Captain Baldwin was silent. Looking up, the girls saw tears running down his cheeks. He rose up, and without a word went out of the room.

But the one that interested us the most was Captain Kennedy, also from the navy, I think. He brought his daughter, a child about Fonnie's age. "Trip," her father called her. She was very slight, her dark hair was shingled. He eyes fairly danced. We were delighted with her. Captain Kennedy had married a Northern woman, and when he resigned she refused to come with him. Captain Kennedy said they allowed the children to decide for themselves what they should do. The younger, a boy, stayed with his mother. Trip came with her father. She was a furious Southerner. She was very ready to express her views, and talked so cleverly and charmingly that everyone stopped to listen to her. Her father said he had had a time getting her through the lines. He said he had to send her to bed more than once to keep her from getting him arrested.

After the War was over, my sisters met in Baltimore an officer in the United States Army who told them that as a Yankee spy he had come through Tappahannock, had spent the night at our house, and our Father had sent him on to Richmond. He was so minute in his description of everybody and everything in our household that my sisters felt sure he was telling the truth.

All this time the Fifty-fifth was being drilled and disciplined. Mr. Austen Brockenbrough and Mr. Lal Roane had gotten the Jefferson Davis Rifles into splendid condition. Once, when one of the Rifles was on picket duty, my Father, to try him, went over the stations after nightfall. He started to cross the sentinel's beat without speaking, but was halted.

"Come, now," my Father said, "you know who I am. You don't need the countersign from me."

"Yes, I does, Major," said the man in great excitement. "My orders is that I shall stop anybody who doesn't give me the countersign, no matter who it is."

"Nonsense," said Father, and he started to go past; but the sentinel stopped him with his lowered gun.

"Now, Major, please, Sir," he said in an agony. "If you goes one step farther, Sir, I am going to shoot you, Sir. Indeed I is."

My Father found his sentinel was in dead earnest. He stood still and praised the soldier, telling him he had done his duty exactly. They had become a fine body of men.

School was over for the present. Midsummer was upon us. Charley, supposed to be at Bladensfield, was very often in Tappahannock. One day he and Harry were out in a little boat fishing with a net. They saw a large eagle—a regular bald-headed United States–flag eagle—flying up from the water a little way, but always descending again. The boys were curious. They sailed closer and saw that the eagle had taken a fish too heavy for him, and could not carry it off. The boys sailed closer still, but the eagle was so engrossed in its efforts to carry off the fish that he paid no attention. They threw the net, enclosed both eagle and fish, and cautiously drew them into the boat. With such a remarkable catch, the boys concluded to come home. They brought their boat to shore, where, with the help of two or three idle soldiers, they got the eagle to land, holding his two immense wings outstretched to prevent him from biting. In this way they walked him up to our lot, followed by an admiring throng of all the idlers on the street.

The boys put the eagle into a large chicken coop near the kitchen and fed him with the fish that had caused his capture. The boys on the street would fish for hours to have the pleasure of feeding him. Sometimes they brought fish, sometimes, to our horror, it was the cats they found on the street. It was terrible to watch the eagle's method of feeding on cats. Unless it was a very tough old tom, he simply cut it in half with his sharp beak, and it was gone in a twinkling.

After a week or two, he would not eat a mouthful. Charley and Harry were worried. They said it was because he was confined. But what was to be done? They clipped one wing and turned him loose in the garden. That utterly destroyed our peace of mind. We were "as afraid of him as of death." When we saw him standing up straight and tall, his wings tightly folded around his body and his fierce eyes flashing around, we never went near that part of the garden, no matter how desirable it might be for flower dolls or play of any kind.

We remembered the story in *McGuffey's Reader* of the Swiss woman whose little boy had been carried off by an eagle to his crag in the high Alps, and how for years she had worked with the little blue jacket fluttering in her sight. Indeed, one of the first things our eagle did was try to pounce upon Silvie's little brown baby in his cradle in front of the kitchen door. Our shrieks brought out Silvie with her broomstick to beat him off before he quite reached the cradle, but the thrill remained with us. Not many days after he was let loose, one of our cats unluckily crossed his path, was pounced upon, divided, and eaten in a moment. We did manage by diligence to save our pet, Matty Matthias. Matty Matthias had a great history. One night quite late after we had gone to bed, our Brother Will came home on a furlough. Of course, I was hard to rouse, but Will had taken me up. I waked sitting in his lap, holding a little white kitten in my arms. All the family was pressed up against Will. He had been in the fighting at Matthias Point, though as I remember, only in the reserve forces. Will looked big and strong in his undress gray uniform. He had grown a little mustache, too. To think of his actually having been in a battle! We felt so proud of him. He told us that in the midst of the fighting this kitten had run out, no one knew from where. Will picked it up and put it in the breast of his coat. The kitten was our darling. We were quite determined the eagle should not devour her. Yet her fate was sad. Harry used to let her sleep in his bed at night, and one night when he was sleeping heavily, he rolled over on her and smothered her. We were greatly distressed, but Harry felt so dreadfully about it we had to make as little of it as we could.

The eagle looked very lonely and very grand, stalking about the garden. Though we were afraid, we couldn't help watching him. After he found he couldn't fly, he never tried to do it—just walked around with his wings pressed close, his fierce eyes taking in everything. We thought he looked scornfully at us, but he never uttered a cry of any kind in complaint.

One morning there were two eagles walking together. A friend had come to visit our prisoner. The two walked around side by side. They seemed to be talking together. Then the visiting eagle would fly up and light on a tree or take a swoop around the sky, as though he were trying to encourage his friend to do the same. Then he would light in the garden and the two would walk around together. About sundown the strange eagle flew away. The next morning our eagle was lying dead under a rosebush. We wondered if the strange eagle had brought his friend some kind of poison, or whether the prisoner had died of a broken heart. His fate made a deep impression on us. Even the baby, who was beginning to talk now, wanted to have the story told him over and over again and used to be put to sleep with a little song about how "the old eagle died under the bush in the garden."

The summer went, and the fall. In the winter our Father, coming from Fort Lowery, told us that little Anton, who had made such a brave cheerful soldier that everyone thought well of him, was ill of a fever. He couldn't eat anything the soldiers brought him. He said if he had one of "Mrs. Ward's rolls" he thought he could eat that. My Mother put up some rolls and whatever else that she thought would tempt him. The Major took it to him, and said, "Anton, here is Mrs. Ward's roll. You must eat that."

The boy held it in his hand, but he looked up at the Major with a little smile and shook his head. He died that night.

I don't remember much about that winter. Strangers still came in great numbers; we had lessons and play. Soldiers came up every evening; the morning's mail brought notes for the grown-up sisters that caused quite a good deal of fluttering. As I remember, they were about engagements for walks and for seances of various kinds. Cousin Philip Lewis always came to see our sister Eddie. Sister Matty had her specials. As for Mamie, she was gay, always talking and laughing, always full of pranks. I wouldn't like to have to name the young soldiers who were her followers. She played off one against another and had the time of her life. All of this was of great interest to Stell and me.

The girls were so taken up with their soldier friends that they neglected the help they should have given their Mother; but thirteen-year-old Lucy stood by her always. Lucy was a tomboy, and the best leader in play that children ever had, but she was also a good little girl of the Sunday-school books. She never failed to tend to breakfast, dinner, and supper, seeing that everything was just as it should be, and to help with the baby and Chan when Louisa was busy. I can see her little workbasket now, so neat and filled with stockings and socks to be darned. Once when Brother Will came home, he noticed her helpful ways and said to her, "That is right, Lucy. You stand by Mamma. She deserves everything we can do for her."

I have often heard Lucy say, even after she grew old, that that commendation from the brother we loved so dearly more than paid for any effort she had made. Will was only twenty-one then, but he seemed like a man in his thirties.

Once in a while now we began to hear of battles, but they seemed far away to us. The big battle of Bull Run, or Manassas, had been fought in July. I don't remember that I cared much about it, but the grownups were electrified. All the men except the very old ones were in the army now; all the women belonged to the Soldier's Aid Society. They scraped lint, made bandages from morning till night.

The "Boys" of the Fifty-fifth had gotten together and had chosen their officers from among their own number. Both of our brothers enlisted as privates. Our parlor was filled every day by privates and officers, and there was no difference made between them. The privates of the Fifty-fifth had come from nearby plantations. Many of them, at their own expense, kept

William N. Ward and Martha Ward ("Brother Will" and "Sister Matty").

horses at Fort Lowery, and a Negro man from the home farm to attend to horse and master. How unlike it must have been to anything that an officer of the regular army was accustomed to deal with! It must have required great tact. Yet I never heard of any insubordination.

It was about this time that two Northern soldiers escaped from prison in Richmond and were traced to the big swamp near Tappahannock called the Slash. A detail of our soldiers was sent out to find them, and find them they did, a little before sundown. We were up on the paling watching when the poor fellows were marched in to the town to be put in the jail for the night. They were young men, very tired and worn looking from what they had gone through. One of them called out to Chan, who was on the paling gazing at them, "Say, Bub, want to see a Yankee?"

We certainly did. I remember to this day the curious sensation I had that they couldn't really be people that would come down to fight and kill our friends and neighbors. But our Mother felt that they were really people. She said, "Poor young things, striving for their freedom!"

When she heard that the sharp slash grass had cut to pieces not only their clothes but their flesh as well, she sent over to them shirts and drawers that belonged to our boys; and Little Phil, the manservant, was made to take over warm water and healing stuffs and bathe and anoint the cut flesh. Somebody objected: "Mrs. Ward, that is no way to treat Yankees, now."

But my Mother answered, "To me they are just two poor boys, cut and suffering, and trying to gain their freedom."

Next there was a rumor that Yankee gunboats were coming up the river. Rifles for the Regiment had come and were in long boxes under Mother's bed. Soldiers were sent up in a great hurry to get them. The soldiers came while my Mother was dressing and burst into her room while she was taking her bath. She cried out and wrapped her towels around herself, but the men said, "No time for modesty now, Madam," and dove under the bed for the box of rifles.

The boxes were opened in our hall, the rifles taken out and stacked in the boats to go to Fort Lowery. Mamma had the long boxes stowed away. Coming back to Bladensfield, she used them for packing cases first, then, turning them bottom upward, she made long mattresses to fit and covered them for lounges. They are the lounges you sit on every day, children, one in the hall, and the other in the dining room.

The gunboats did not come very far up river. I think everything was going toward Richmond at that time.

Then the order came for the Fifty-fifth to join its army corps. Everyone in Tappahannock was deeply moved. The Regiment left Fort Lowery and camped for the night just outside the village. Our Mother took us to see the encampment just as the men were getting ready for supper. We went from squad to squad to see the bustle of supper cooking and the men sitting around in circles to eat it. Before we left, the camp was lighted up. It was a pretty sight, but Mother was sad and depressed. True, neither of her boys was going, and Father was to give up his command as soon as the Regiment reached Richmond, but the soldiers were our neighbors and friends, and it was said they were to be sent immediately into battle. Our Will was already at the front.

The next morning, early, the Regiment and the cavalry troop came into Tappahannock and broke ranks for a few moments to say good-bye. I shall never forget that scene. You may be sure everybody was there. There were good-byes and cheery words—no tears. Then the drums beat for formation. There was a moment of stir; then silence; then the order, "Forward march!"

I can never forget that silence, nor the scrape of feet as the column moved down the silent street. The women on the sidewalks waved and smiled encouragement though there were tears running down their cheeks. Not even a child made a sound. Tom Gordon was marching with an extra pair of shoes hanging down his back over his knapsack. The Regiment was gone! It left a sad little town behind it.

Father had fever and did not go with the Regiment. The doctor had ordered him to bed. He was to leave as soon as he was well enough to be about.

Upstairs in the garret Harry's stump-tailed tabby cat had one kitten about a month old. That night she brought it down and laid it close up against Father's back in the bed. We thought that was very clever of her. She had put her kitten as close as she could to the only soldier left in the town.

There were rumors of Yankee gunboats on the river. The town was so uneasy that no grown people undressed. In the morning early, Chan, who had dressed and gone out, came running back. Mamma was saying her prayers. She always prayed a very long time, it seemed to us, and her prayers seemed to grow longer and longer. Chan waited for her a little while, then pulled her dress, and said, "Mamma, you'd better stop saying your prayers and get up. The Yankees are nearly here."

You may believe she got up quickly. It was true: the gunboats were already at Fort Lowery. The report was that as soon as they had destroyed the Fort, they were coming up to shell Tappahannock. Things began to move. Blind old Dr. Roane was driven away in his carriage. He held between his knees his greatest treasure, the portrait of the wife he had loved so devotedly. She had died very young, leaving him his two sons, Tom and Lal. They and her memory had made the Doctor's life. We wondered what would become of the silver and the handsome furnishings of the big Roane House, for the Doctor was the rich man of the village.

My father was wrapped in blankets and taken to the house of some friends in the country. Mamie went with him. Mother, Sister Matty, and whoever was able to help were busy packing up our things, for we were going back to Bladensfield. As the intention to go back to Bladensfield had been in mind since the Regiment had received marching orders, a good many of our things had already been sent on, but there was a great deal still to go.

Boom!—a great sound like very loud thunder! It was the blasting of the Fort. That stirred things up still more. We knew that as soon as the Fort was blown up, the gunboats would come up to the village. People said they might be there at any moment.

"The children must be put in safety," said Mamma. "I can't work knowing they may be killed by a shell at any moment."

We begged to stay till she could come with us.

"No," said Mamma, "you must go now."

We put on our wraps. It was March, but bright and sunny, not very cold. Eddie got the baby and Chan ready and we started out to go to Greenfield, the Brockenbrough's farm near Tappahannock. Poor Eddie had big Ran, now nearly two years old, in her arms and Chan clinging to her hand. Stell, Fonnie, and I and all of the little blacks, Silvie's children, followed behind. Lucy and Louisa were to follow after they had got ready some lunch. I can see us now, struggling down the street and over the fields, scared to death. As we came out on a hill overlooking the river, a gunboat hove in sight and steamed up to the foot of Main Street—a pretty sight, but terrible to us. We began to run. Chan's shoe came off in the mud. We had to stop to put it on. Across the field we saw Lucy, Louisa, and Jack, the fly-brush boy, struggling against the wind to get to us.

We had hardly got started again when, *Boom!* came a great noise from the gunboat. Every one of us dropped to the ground, flat, and lay there. Lucy, seeing us drop, thought we were all killed. Indeed, we almost thought so ourselves. She hurried to us, found us lying flat—Eddie, too, for she suffered with fright—but none of us in the least hurt.

We sat there for some time. No other gun was fired. Indeed, we learned afterward that the one that frightened us so had only a blank cartridge. Lucy insisted that we go farther from the river. There was an old barn and stable toward the woods. We got up and went skedaddling to it. There was a horse in a stall in the stable and a quantity of fodder on the floor in the adjoining barn. We sat down on the fodder and Lucy talked and even laughed, but I was like Eddie, I was scared. I saw nothing to laugh at in the situation. I remember that every time the old horse tugged at his bundle of fodder and made a rustling noise, I shuddered with fear. Eddie was almost whimpering. Presently we heard a long drawn-out cry.

"Oh!" cried Eddie, "Lucy, Lucy! That was Ma. That was her voice!"

"Pshaw," said Lucy, "Mamma! It was nothing but an old cow mooing." No doubt that is what it was.

We stayed in the barn till it began to be late, then ate our lunch, then waited again, then as no one came to us, we picked ourselves up and went home. There we found almost everything packed up. The house was dismantled. To the grownups, no doubt, it looked gloomy and forlorn, but children are such odd contraptions that anything that is a change goes fairly well with them. One doesn't have to be careful in a dismantled house, and we were delighted at the thought of going back to Bladensfield.

The strange thing was to see the Yankees walking about the streets. It seemed to us that, like portfire, they would cause conflagration where they went, but they passed and repassed harmlessly. They were looking for our Father, but at our door, they got no information. That night we were tired and slept soundly, but it was an anxious time for the grownups. The Yankees were all around our house keeping watch and walking through the porches. We supposed they thought our Father might come home after nightfall.

In the morning Mamie came back. She told us that Father's fever was lower and that he was comfortable and well cared for by his friends.

Soon after her arrival, Mamie received a note from Cousin Philip Lewis telling her that he had been sent to find out how many Yankees were at Tappahannock, who was their commander, and any other information possible about them. He wrote that he was hiding behind the chimney of the old Presbyterian church, and asked if she could help him. I don't remember who brought the note. Mamie wrote on a scrap of paper that she could find out what he asked for, and would send him a note as soon as possible. Harry was a big boy then—thirteen years old. He went down among the Yankees seeing and asking what questions he dared. He was a shrewd boy. When he came back, he told how many gunboats there were, about how many men, and that the boats were under the command of Captain McCray. I don't know that I am spelling the name correctly.

Mamie wrote down what he told her and sent Jack the fly-brush boy to carry the note to Cousin Philip. We climbed up on the althea hedge, and from there we could see Jack going. We could see the old ivy-covered chimney, too.

Presently there was some commotion among the Yankees. One band formed and marched up Main Street before our house, another up the back street between our house and Dr. Roane's. The old church was between those streets farther down. Mamie came into the garden, pale enough, but trying to seem as usual. Then everybody came out to watch. We knew the Yankees had got wind of Cousin Philip's being there and were out to take him. We couldn't see Cousin Philip, but Jack told us he was scratching a note on the pommel of his saddle when he looked up and saw the Yankees coming. He crammed the paper into his pocket, put spurs to his horse, and away he went. It was well his horse was a good one and that Cousin Philip was a good horseman. They said the horse skimmed the ground like a flying squirrel. The Yankees changed to a double-quick.

"Shoot him! Shoot him!" some of them cried.

"No, take him alive," someone else called.

"Halt!" came the order.

Cousin Philip turned in his saddle to wave his hand.

"No halt in me, gentlemen," his voice came back.

He was soon flying over the Long Bridge, and reached camp safely with Mamie's note in his pocket.

It stirred our blood to see that young fellow riding so gallantly for his life. We were beginning to know something about war.

That evening Mamie went back to Papa. Mamma sent Harry down to ask Captain McCray whether she might be allowed to cross the river with her family and effects. He sent her a very courteous answer: that while he was in command he would see that she was allowed to cross without molestation, but that he expected to go very shortly and could not answer for those who came after him. He said it would be well for us to go as soon as possible. Captain McCray was a Southern man, an officer in the navy who had not come South.

*Lucy, Charles, and Harry
left to right.*

Mamma decided that we children should go the next day. She sent a letter that night to Charley at Bladensfield to be at the Ferry with the carriage to meet us.

That evening the gunboats sailed away. There were no longer any Yankees in Tappahannock, but we hurried because Captain McCray said others were coming. We made an odd-looking procession going down to the boat in the morning. Everyone carried something. Harry had his cat and her kitten in a basket. I had some newly hatched chickens in my pretty black-and-white split basket. On top of the basket was the bamboo mat that went under the tea waiter at the table, and on the mat was my dear big doll, Lucy. I held the handle of the basket on my arm.

Sister Matty, Eddie, Lucy, and Harry, and Louisa with Silvie's (the cook's) two children, Maria and Frank. Silvie was to stay till Mamma could come, which would not be till our Father was well enough to go to his command. At the last moment an orphan child about Stell's age was brought to cross with us and to be put in the care of her guardian at Warsaw. She was a harmless little creature, a little conceited and given to talkativeness. My mother felt very pityingly toward her, an orphan, tossed around with no one but a guardian to care for her, but we took an unreasoning dislike to her. We insisted that this Eliza Brooks had a smell about her we didn't like, and we didn't want her to sit by us. Our mother scolded us and made us treat her politely, but she couldn't make us like her.

It was a very bright, sunny morning in March, the Saturday before Easter. Big, fat Uncle John Leverpool, as black as he could be, and his brother, Uncle Edward, were the ferrymen. They were both very kind and very reliable. The crossing was delightful. Not a sign of gunboats either up or down the beautiful river stretching out around us. Everything went well, but when we reached the other side there were no Charley and no carriage to meet us.

Sister Matty said, "Never mind." Anything might have delayed him. But she asked a boy who had come over with us if he would ride into Bladensfield and tell Charley we had crossed. The Ferry was only ten miles from Bladensfield and the boy had to pass our gate. He promised faithfully he would see Charley and tell him we were at the Ferry.

We were not anxious at all. We ran up and down the shore, picked up stones, and played in the sand. No one lived at the Ferry, not even Uncle John and Uncle Edward, but there was an old deserted cabin with a broken bedstead in one corner. Louisa put Ran to sleep for his morning nap on a shawl spread on the planks of the bedstead, and Sister Matty and Eddie found an old box they could use for a chair when they tired of the shore.

The sky began to cloud and the wind rose, chill and bleak. Sister Matty and Eddie began to grow anxious, but we still played on the shore. Uncle John and Uncle Ned had made another trip and were not going again that day unless they were signaled. Twilight began to fall. They put up their boat for the night and Uncle Ned went home, but kind Uncle John stayed with us. By this time all of us wished we were at Bladensfield, but still there was no Charley with the carriage. It was growing dark. The river was black and the waves rose and whipped the shore. Lucy took out the candles to make light. There wasn't a match! Then we did feel badly. And from down the darkening river came the big blowing of a gunboat. Yankees!

"Uncle John," said Sister Matty, "you can't stay here all night. You must go home, and do, pray, get someone to come for us."

Uncle John knew she was right. When she asked him, he unbound our rolled-up mattress and spread it on the old bedstead, told us good night, and left.

Out on the river there were several gunboats. We could tell that by the different sounds of the whistles. We were scared enough now in the dark. Eddie was almost wringing her hands, but Sister Matty and Lucy were brave and cheerful. We tried to be the same.

"It is rather good we have no matches," said Lucy. "If there was a light, the Yankees might come to see what was here."

Sister Matty made us lie down on the one bed, and laid our coats over us, for the night was black and chill. There were so many for one bed! We were very wriggly. None of us wanted to lie by poor Eliza Brooks. I think we were very hard-hearted. However, we did it, and didn't complain of her smell. Little Maria and Frank, the colored children, had the mattress cover folded up for them, and with their wrappings over them they were soon sound asleep.

Baby Ran was not in the least pleased. He said, "Dark! Dark!" a good many times. Sister Matty had him in her arms.

"Take Ran in Mamma's room," he begged.

"Dear little Boy, I can't take you there just now," Sister Matty answered.

"Then just take me in the diney room," he sighed.

"You put your head down on my arm and shut your eyes, and just see what you will see!" coaxed Sister Matty.

She began to sing about the old eagle that died under the bush in the garden till the complaints ceased. Ran was asleep. One by one, we on the bed went to sleep too, trying to keep our feet still lest we should make the others wriggle, and holding ourselves carefully away for fear of touching Eliza Brooks. Sister Matty had the box, but Eddie, Lucy, and Louisa had nothing to sit on but the floor. They took uneasy naps with their heads against the wall. The blowing of the gunboats passing up the dark, misty river made them too anxious to sleep.

About midnight, as it seemed to us—it might not have been so late—a great pounding at the door brought us all up standing. Louisa ran to the door and held it shut. "Who is there?" she called.

The door was partly pushed open in spite of her force and a man's voice said, "A friend. Girl, open the door!"

"It is Mr. Brockenbrough, Louisa. It is Mr. Brockenbrough," cried Sister Matty. "Don't you hear his voice? Open the door."

It was pushed open with a decisive motion, and big, bluff, splendid-looking Mr. Waller Brockenbrough came in, his quick, black eyes, like eagles' eyes, taking in everything. He put out his arms and gathered us in. I never thought one man's arms could take in so many. Eagles' eyes? But such kind eagles' eyes! They were shining through tears as he held us, and said, "Poor children!"

Mr. Waller Brockenbrough was a bachelor, just beginning not to be young, who lived all alone on his plantation some miles up the river from the Ferry. Uncle John had gone home, eaten his supper, then gone to Mr. Brockenbrough's house to tell him of our plight. The spring rains had left the roads through the Rappahannock flats in a terrible condition. All of this had caused delay, but at last here Mr. Brockenbrough was with a big farm wagon well lined with straw.

We were piled in, one after another.

"Now," called Mr. Brockenbrough, "are all in?"

"I ain't," came a voice from the darkness. It was poor little Maria, who was about to be forgotten.

At last we were off. There was thick darkness everywhere, and rain was falling. Mr. Brockenbrough had brought a man on horseback with a lantern, who was to go ahead of us to find and warn his master of the dangerous holes in the road. We went slowly, the horses sometimes pulling their feet out of the mud with a sucking sound, and we were thankful when we drew up in front of Mr. Brockenbrough's door. A servant with a light came out to meet us. The door was thrown open wide. Things looked bright and cheerful inside. Soon we were standing before a big log fire whose flame was filling the chimney and a pleasant-looking yellow woman was putting supper on the table.

Mr. Brockenbrough sat at the foot of the table, ample and hospitable, as Sister Matty poured coffee at the head. Everything was in abundance and excellent of its kind, and we were all hungry. The grownups were laughing and talking and telling experiences, but as soon as we were through with supper, we began to nod. It was late. All of us went upstairs together. There we found one room nicely furnished. There were two double beds. On the floor in the next room was pallet after pallet. Oh! Such pallets! Soft and warm, made entirely of blankets. I never knew any one household to have so many blankets. Later the Yankees took every one—looted the house. We fell asleep as soon as we touched our beds, and did not waken till the sun was shining the next morning.

It was Easter. I well remember the day, shifty and chill—sometimes a cold gleam of sun, sometimes cloudy. After breakfast Sister Matty and Eddie talked with Mr. Brockenbrough by the fire. We felt like fish out of water and did not know what to do. The peach trees were in bloom, but there was not much fun in being out, such a cold wind flapped us about.

I remember the dinner we had because it was served so unusually. On a large flat dish were turnip greens, and on that a hot boiled ham surrounded by, alternately, corn meal dumplings and poached eggs. It looked queer to us, but was all good. Every one of us was fond of turnip greens. The ham was an old one, and delicious. Looking back, I think Bachelor Mr. Brockenbrough's yellow housekeeper did wonderfully well, with all of us turned in on her in the middle of the night.

The weather being very bad, we spent Sunday night also with Mr. Brockenbrough. Early Monday morning some kind friends from Warsaw had heard of our plight, and sent down to bring us to their houses. Mr. Brockenbrough took Sister Matty and the baby in his buggy and left them at the house of Mr. Thomas Jones, where Louisa and I were waiting for them. Mrs. Shackleford took the rest to her hospitable house.

The Joneses were dear friends of ours. No one could have been kinder to us than they were, but there were only grown-up people there, except one big boy, too old to want to talk to me. I had a sedate time looking at pictures and books. At the Shacklefords' was a welter of children. I longed to be in the fray. After breakfast Louisa took the baby and me around there to stay awhile, coming back to the Joneses' for dinner. I found nothing sedate in the nursery at the Shacklefords'. The Shackleford children had threatened to shut up our little black Maria in a large screen and said they were going to press her flat. Of course, they would never have hurt her, but Stell and Fonnie were fierce in defense of their little black friend. In the fray, Stell's big doll, Molly, the only big doll she ever had, had been broken across her shoulder. Children: Molly is upstairs in the bureau drawer now. You may go up and look at her head (the rats have eaten up her bran body), and run your fingers over the place on her shoulder where Lucy mended her with glue that morning.

Much of the pleasure of Fonnie's young life and mine—dear Stell did not live to be grown—came from the Jones and the Shackleford households. The memory of them comes back to me with warm affection—the pranks and warm-hearted gaiety of the Shackleford young people, with the sympathetic background of their mother's cordiality. As for the Joneses, the many evenings we spent with them, the books we read and discussed together, the nights they took us in after dances in the neighborhood when perhaps the house was crowded are memories I can never part with.

Mamma had come, and next morning Charley came with the carriage and wagon and we went out to Bladensfield. Willie Jones drove Mamma, Louisa, Sister Matty, the baby and me in the Joneses' carriage. It was lovely to see the dear woods again, to drive under the big oaks, all of them misty with the promise of spring, and then to be back at home with Aunt Eve and Amy smiling their welcome. We had to run all over the house first, then the woods, to make sure it was real. The rooms each seemed to welcome us. Even our two little vases on the nursery mantlepiece that we had felt concerned about not taking away with us stood there waiting. We ran down to drink from the spring that has always been famous for its sparkling purity; then to Arbutus Hill to see if the arbutus was in bloom; then to look at the minnows in the stream. It was lovely to be back at home again.

Things dropped back into the old ways. We had lessons by ourselves again up in the nursery with Sister Matty for our teacher; we had our own little gardens down by the big apple tree and went into the woods to make chestnut whistles and catch minnows. Later, the bees swarmed a good many times. Mamma would be out cutting asparagus and would be the first to see them. She would call and begin to beat on her pan with the knife she was using for the asparagus. Maybe we had grown drowsy over lessons upstairs, but all must run when the bees swarmed. We would get the bell, pans, the waiter—everything that could be beaten on to make a noise. There we would be making pandemonium in the sunshine till the bees were well settled.

"One of the very old places in Virginia."

While in Tappahannock we had almost forgotten the Pecks.

In *The Journal and Letters of Philip Vickers Fithian* he tells that when he gave up his position as tutor at Nomini Hall, he put in his place his friend, Mr. Peck. Later Mr. Peck married his pupil, Ann Tasker Carter. Bladensfield was their home. Your Great-Grandfather bought it from their daughter, and all of the Peck family lie buried in the Old Peck Graveyard down below the garden. When you stand in the south door and look down the garden walk, you see the handsome group of the graveyard trees. It looked very lovely this spring with the dogwood and the yellow sassafras blooming among the dark pines and cedars. It is carpeted with periwinkles. We used to look at them, but never pulled them. Mamma wouldn't let us. "They were put there for poor dead people," she said.

Very quiet the graves looked, lying in the sunshine, but the servants used to tell us stories of the ghosts of the people buried there; how they came out at night and walked about their old haunts. Mr. Peck, the servants said, had been a very severe master. They were sure he had gone to "the bad places." They used to tell us of seeing him at night in the studio which had been his study. They said he smelled of sulphur and that a great flame of fire flared out from his breast.

The ghost we loved was a sweet Miss Alice Peck, the last one buried in the graveyard. Her rosebush still bloomed in the garden. The servants told stories of her loveliness and goodness; of the lover who hung over her as she lay dying in the room over the parlor. They said she could not rest, but was always coming back because he still lived, and she had to watch over him.

Old Aunt Amy Fauntleroy, a very old colored woman, said when she was a little girl, before we lived at Bladensfield, the ghosts were so troublesome that Captain and Mrs. Davis had to have them "laid." Aunt Amy said she was at the Laying. She said a Baptist minister came out to the graveyard wearing his coat inside out and upside down. He walked backward and read a chapter of the Bible, reading from the bottom of the page to the top. Aunt Amy said, "Ef yer hadn't er knowed it was the Bible, yer'd er thought it was pu-o nonsense." But she said the ghosts were never so bad after that. She said, "All the colored people, far an' near, came, an' arter that they wa'nt so feared 'cause dey knowed de ghosses wuz laid."

Mamma did not like us to hear these stories. She told us not to believe them. We thought we didn't; only we loved to play about Miss Alice and make believe in the daytime. When twilight began to make the far corners of the halls and stairways dim and mysterious, we used to go running noiselessly to where the grown people were, looking backward as we went with a feeling that something not of earth was behind us.

The Short Room in our garret, where we played so often, should have been called the third story, for then it was neatly plastered. The Long Room, the size of four of our downstairs rooms, was generally kept locked. There, before the War, were kept the barrel of brown sugar, the cones of loaf sugar, jars of dried cherries, demijohns of blackberry wine, bags of dried fruit, of chestnuts, and sundry other supplies. In summer, on the north side, the winter garments of the family hung from hooks by the dormer windows. The quilting frame was there; the candle molds hung by the windows. That was where the winding blades lived when they were not being used. There was a long box filled with clothes that had belonged to generations before us. There were any number of poke bonnets, and one dear little Dunstable made of drawn blue silk. There was a lovely brown brocade silk mantle that Mamma used to wear years before, and there were men's coats and trousers. When we had to stay in on account of the weather, we were allowed to dress up in these things. If we made too much noise, Louisa would be sent up to quiet us.

We loved to be there in broad daylight, but for no reason on earth, when the twilight began to fall, we were afraid. The clothes, hanging from the hooks by the windows, swayed. We would remember what the servants had told us about the Pecks, who had lived at Bladensfield before us.

The Short Room wasn't quite so bad, though I liked it only in broad daylight. That was where we children, whites and blacks, got out the radish seed for the next seeding; the mustard, coriander, and fennel. We shelled great numbers of snap beans and peas up there. We had a way of playing with the beans as though they were people—today I can hardly see how we could have done it—and we laughed and sang and had great times, so long as it was daylight.

The little south room, so full of sunlight, was our own playroom where lived our dolls, china and rag, and where the Baby House was.

Once in a while, Mamma would say, "Children, I want you to sweep out the Long Room today and put it in good order. When you have finished, I will come up to see how nicely you have done it."

We loved that. We loved to peek at and play with all the old things. There were old books up there: Papa's pile of *The Spirit of Missions,* a few copies of *The Southern Literary Messenger,* and some old novels whose backs were ragged.

Most of the children of Bladensfield could draw. When they saw anything, they could make a picture of it. Old Mr. Michelli, a stranded old French artist (his name was Italian, but he called himself a Frenchman and spoke French), whom my Father had found and persuaded to live at Bladensfield, taught drawing and French to us and to the youth of the Northern Neck generally. He was pleased and encouraged by the progress made by his Bladensfield pupils until he came to Eddie. Teddie, our Father called her. She was only a little girl then. One day Eddie was working hard over the drawing of a dog's head. She felt rather pleased with her success. Mr. Michelli leaned over to correct her work. He took his crayon and scratched the dog's head out.

"Oh, Teddie, Teddie," he said. "Sorry dog, sorry dog! You go practice your music."

Poor Eddie! She wept, and never tried to draw again. She knew that Mr. Tepe, who taught her music, thought she was far and away beyond all his other pupils, but that did not console her in the least. All the others could learn to draw. She could not! That seemed to give her a sense of inferiority that she never lost. Her music was her delight, her passion, but it never, in her eyes, lifted her to the plane of those who could draw. If Sister Matty drew her a spray of wild roses or morning-glories twining up a hollyhock stalk, or Mamie made a sketch of Eddie that really showed a likeness, Eddie treasured them as works of art. She thought nothing of it that her music made people stand still and forget themselves and go on their way with hearts full of emotion.

Mother used to tell us that when Eddie was a bit of a baby, learning to kneel down and hide her eyes with her baby hands, one day at prayers, our Father read from *Thornton's Family Prayers,* "Exercise us in all Godliness." Eddie sprang from her knees and spun round and round, singing, "Exercise and hooks and eyes; and hooks and eyes and exercise." That was the first evidence of her sense of sound. When she was only three years old, Mamma said she used to sing "The Star-Spangled Banner," clapping her fat little legs for accompaniment, while the grownups of her generation stood around to applaud. She was an almost-grown-up Eddie when I can first remember her, making music for us daily on the piano.

Mr. Tepe was another find of our Father's. He was a German student who had been banished from his country for joining in a student rebellion. He landed in New York without money and could not speak a word of English. Fortunately, the piano is understood by Americans and Germans alike. Somewhere there was a piano on which this forlorn young student was pouring out his feelings, when a gentleman from Washington who was looking for a music teacher for his daughters heard him. Fortunately, again, this gentleman spoke German. He brought Mr. Tepe to Washington, where he might have remained but for his inability to keep from making love to his pupils. He was soon stranded again, only a little less forlorn because he had picked up a few words of English.

When he was beginning to wonder if shooting himself might not be the only way out, my Father found him and brought him to Bladensfield, to teach music to the children there for his board and a small salary, and to build up a class in the neighborhood. At Bladensfield he seems to have lived a happy and successful life. I say "seems," for this is legend to me. I was the baby then, and Fonnie, Chan, and Ran were still in Heaven.

Mr. Tepe must have been a pleasant, lovable fellow. Evidently, our Mother petted him, made him at home and teased him, too, sometimes. I used to hear of his looking into the kitchen window before starting out on his round of lessons to tell the cook, "Sibie, be sure to have me some cabbage tonight, fried good and brown."

Years after he had gone, there was a pretty old black Wedgwood teapot with a broken spout, which was called "Mr. Tepe's teapot" because he always used it when he went blackberrying with the family.

Mamma used to tell us that once when she was labeling some of his new collars, she wrote on one of them his name in full—Francis Arnold Theodore Joseph Aloysius Hemis Tepe—it went entirely around the band of the collar. He took it as a joke, but never would wear the collar.

Mr. Tepe lived at Bladensfield several years, but his inveterate habit of making love to his pupils got the better of him at last. When irascible Mr. Frederick Brown of Peccatone found him embracing his pretty daughter and kicked him up from the piano, he moved to some town in Mississippi, from which place we heard from him for some years. He prospered, married (a pupil, of course), and was living there the last we knew.

Of his pupils at Bladensfield, Sister Matty worked hard and learned to play some difficult pieces brilliantly. Mamie loved songs best, which she sang very sentimentally. Eddie filled the house with her music at all times of the day. Now she was teaching us. Already it was pleasant to hear Stell's scales and exercises coming out of the parlor. I learned slowly. Fonnie was too young to begin.

Back at Bladensfield, going our old ways, it hardly seemed possible that war was going on, although our Father was still in Richmond on official business. It was during this spring that our Will was elected captain of his company. The Virginia regiments recruited for the War had gotten together and from themselves had elected their own officers. Mr. John Lyell had been chosen captain of Will's company; now he was made colonel of the Regiment and Will was elected to fill his place. Of course we were delighted. I think our poor dear Mother thought perhaps Will's life might be easier—even safer. She was mistaken in this.

About this time—it might have been before or after, I can't remember —Charley went to Warsaw for the mail and came scurrying back. The village was full of Yankees! I was all of a tremble. I know Eddie was too, for she was timid like me, but Mamie and Lucy seemed only excited. We did not know what to expect. Mamma wouldn't let a light be carried in the front part of the house, and no one undressed that night. We children went to sleep in our clothes on top of the bedclothes to waken in the middle of the night and find the grown people up, eating a little improvised meal.

The night passed quietly—no disturbance of any kind. Our neighbors said afterward they thought it was because we were so far in the woods. They said the Yankees had been attacked higher up the Neck by "bushwhackers," and seemed to be on the lookout for them.

Everything was quiet. Toward sundown the next day, Harry went to shoot bullfrogs on the big ice pond near the main road. He had shot several and was taking aim when he saw a squad of Yankees riding by. He kept still, but the Yankees saw him. The officer rode close to the fence and looked over. "Bub," he said, "you must be a Frenchman—shooting frogs."

Then they passed on. Harry came home with his frogs to tell his tale. He had met the Yankees alone, and was alive! A few days later we heard they had left the Northern Neck.

At the next meeting of the Soldiers' Aid Society, many of our friends were greatly excited telling about the coming of the Yankees to their houses. They did not seem to have done much harm. They had come for horses. They took every horse they found. After that, nobody's horses stayed in the stables. Ours were stabled every night in different places in the woods. Phil, our leading workman, was very good and faithful.

I must stop here to tell how good and faithful all of our colored people were to us during those four hard years. Papa was away. Will was away. Charley was only a boy. The overseer was drafted and gone, but Phil and Uncle Charles worked more steadily and better than they had ever done. The women were good, too. Even Silvie, the cook, didn't get drunk and didn't fly into a passion with Mamma once. She did waken us one Sunday morning by choking our dear Louisa under the nursery window. It seems they had fought all the way from the kitchen—about twenty yards or more from the house. I believe Silvie would have choked Louisa to death if Charley had not run down to take her away.

Silvie was a character. She drank when she could get the whiskey and was very temperamental. When she was angry, she was a sardonic fiend, but she was the best cook in the neighborhood. Her bread and rolls were my mother's pride. It was the rarest thing in the world they ever failed to be as light as a feather, and they were always baked perfectly dry though without being burned. Some of the credit, I think, belonged to Mamma. In the winter she always kept the bread at night in a warm corner of the dining room where the constant big log fire made a very steady heat, and while we sat around the fire after supper, she would turn the bread jar around and around that all sides might be equally heated. Then early, very early in the morning, Silvie would bring the dough in her big wooden tray up into our Mother's room and work it over by the warm fire. Mamma and Papa would be lying in bed, but if Silvie stopped too soon, Mamma would call out, "Work that bread longer, Silvie."

We loved to get out of bed and come to get little pinches of dough that we worked for ourselves, and made queer-shaped rolls—breastpins—a big roll in the middle and tiny ones around it. We would put them into the pan with Silvie's rolls, and they stayed by our fire till Mamma thought them light enough to be baked.

Silvie was a fine meat cook as well. Indeed, she cooked everything well, but we were rather afraid of her. We did not love her as we did Louisa. Even Silvie's children loved Louisa best. Yet Silvie was generally very good to us, especially in regard to the pinches of dough in the mornings, and she made the best gingerbread that children ever ate. In the fall when she was cooking black-eyed peas she was good, too. We would get

through with our lessons a long time before dinner—three o'clock was our
dinner hour—sometimes it was later. We would take our cups and spoons
(the white children had earthenware mugs and the colored children had
tin cups) to Silvie. She would fill them with the boiled peas before they
were mashed for baking. We had some of the liquor, too. We loved to take
this picnic to the back part of the turkey house where there was a place we
could sit, high up near the eaves. There what laughs and songs we had sitting all in a row!

Sometimes we sang the soldiers' songs about the German recruit who

> "Would put mein frou in breechy-loons
> And go to fight mit Seigle."

Or the Irish soldier,

> "Och! I'm Paddy Whack
> From Ballaminack,
> Not long ago turned soldier—
> To storm the attack, the grand attack
> There's none than I'll be bolder."

Sometimes Amy led in darky hymns:

> "Little Chillun, you'd better believe,
> 'Tis a long time wagging up the cross-roads.

> "Little Chillun, you'd better believe,
> 'Tis a long time wagging up the cross-roads,
> We'll go home by'm bye!"

Or:

> "King! King! Who yer call 'King'?
> I call my Jesus, King of many men."

It was a good many years before we understood that "King of many
men" meant King Emmanuel. As for the hymn beginning "Little Chillun,"
I can't yet think what it did mean, but it sang beautifully. Often we sang
the hymns our Mother had taught us. We were singing children. I believe
singing is good for children; it absorbs their badness.

In 1862 we had a great crop of raspberries and lovely weather for picking them. One beautiful day while we were gathering the berries, we heard a sound like faraway thunder. It came again and again at intervals. Then a strange jarring, trembling sensation. The grown people said it was the discharge of musketry. It was a battle! It might be the beginning of the expected fighting around Richmond. Will was there. No wonder the grown people had drawn, set faces. We little ones picked in silence, thinking of that strange, strange struggle that was going on.

It was the beginning of the seven days' battles around Richmond, though we had no news for several days. It seems almost impossible that we could have heard it on the northern side of the Rappahannock, but we did. We heard it only that day, though the fighting continued for a week.

Then a letter came from Father. Will was wounded. He had been shot in the shoulder as he was cheering his men on in the battle of Gaines's Mill. Mamma was not to be alarmed, the letter said: Will was not in the hospital. Cousin Mary Barney, at whose house Father was staying, had had him brought to her, and he was having the best of care.

Mamma was absolutely quiet. I suppose she had lived over so many times the coming of that message that she could not be said to be alarmed, but she said she must go.

Could she leave Ran? He was only two years old.

"Yes, you, Matty, must take care of him for me."

But how was she to get to Richmond when we were far outside the "Lines," and the Yankee army was between us and Will?

She did not know, but she must go. Sister Matty tried to cheer her: "Will was not severely wounded. Papa said he would soon be well again."

Mamma looked at her as though she had not heard what she said. Taking what little money could be spared, she started. Phil drove her to the Ferry. It was easy to cross the Ferry. Uncle John and Uncle Ned with their boat still plied across, dodging the Yankees when their gunboats were in the river. Across, in Tappahannock, some friends took her farther on. Wherever she stopped, some friend gladly took her in and helped her on her way. Anyone would have done as much for a stranger, if she were a mother going to her wounded son.

Nearing Richmond, there was a little river to cross. I have forgotten which of the little rivers it was. The Yankees had taken all of the boats. Mamma stopped a while at the house of a Mr. Bailor. His boats were all gone. The men on the place had pushed themselves across in an old horse trough, but a lady couldn't go in such a way, he said.

Yes, Mamma said, she could.

Spending the night with Mr. Bailor was a man who should be written about. His name was Camillier or Cameron, I cannot remember which it was, but I think it was Camillier. He was a Northern man of a Scotch family. He thought the war all wrong, and could not bring himself to take either side, but stayed with the fighting wherever it was going on, went on the battlefields, no matter what the danger, to help and bring away the wounded. When he could, he went up and down the country to get fresh eggs, vegetables, and milk for the wounded. He helped either side, but I think most of his time was devoted to our wounded.

Mr. Camillier was to cross that evening rather late, for he had some supplies for his wounded in Richmond, and had to cross the Yankees' lines. He said if Mamma could cross with him, he could drive her into Richmond in the buggy he had waiting on the other side.

Yes, she said, she could cross, and thanked him so much.

When the twilight deepened, they took to the water, Mamma standing, holding to Mr. Camillier in the middle of the trough, a Negro man in one end to push, while a little darky boy with a tin bucket in the other bailed out the water to keep the trough afloat.

The river was very narrow. They had not far to scull. On the far side Mr. Camillier produced his buggy and horse for the rest of the journey. They were in the midst of the battlefields soon. Mr. Camillier had to wait for the moon, and then take a circuitous route to avoid the sentinels. When it was late, they came to the battlefield of Cold Harbor. The wounded had been carried off, but not the dead of either side. As they went slowly and carefully along, Mr. Camillier would say, "Look to the left, Mrs. Ward," when the dead lay in heaps on the right, or, "Now, look to the right," when it was just the other way. It must have been a strange, weird midnight drive, but at last, as the sun rose, they came to Richmond, and soon after, Mamma was by Will's bedside.

Now we waited for letters. They did not come regularly, as the mails could not always get through the Lines, but they brought fairly good news. Will was doing well. The bullet had entered his shoulder and gone somewhere into his breast; Mamma wrote that he was very anxious to have it probed for, but there was a disagreement among the surgeons. The principal one, an old man, insisted upon letting the ball alone, as long as the wound was doing well. The young surgeons were eager to cut it out.

But Will was cheerful and bright, eager for all the company he was allowed to receive, and though he could not write himself, sent us long, saucy messages in Mamma's letters.

At home, we settled down to the queer life without Mamma. The grown sisters were very careful of us. Sister Matty had charge of Ran, the baby, and the housekeeping, and she ran the farm and garden. Little running was needed, with Phil and Uncle Charles to help. Mamie cared for the older children and the fowls. Eddie and Lucy helped in every way. They were all as good as gold, faithful and loving to us.

The fruit began to ripen. It was good-bye to all but the most necessary jobs. Every morning all of us children, from Harry and Jack the fly-brush boy down to Fonnie, went to the orchard and gathered peaches. I remember what an abundant crop we had that year, and what a splendid young orchard. In those days no one in our neighborhood ever sold a peach, but our neighbors and friends would send their wagons, and we gave them all they wanted.

After we had gathered hampers and hampers of peaches, we little girls washed them while the grown people pared. The scaffold in the garden would be covered with driers; and as soon as the first lot was dried it would be covered again. And when the rains came! My! What scampering! We had dried cherries in June, and after the peaches there would be apples and quinces and quantities of preserves, jams, and jellies made from each. The Long Room would be well stocked for winter. Anyone might think that with so much work with peaches we would not have cared to eat them, but it never seemed to have that effect. We children, white and black, took knives with us on our trips to the orchard. I should not like to say how many peaches we ate. The law of the grown people didn't limit us, or any other law except our capacities. The fruit was of the best, and most beautiful.

Chan, who was five years old now, and his boy, Frank, who was Silvie's son, practiced a method of consumption that brought on a tragedy. They went regularly to the orchard, split off the delicious fruit, and cracked and ate the kernel of the stone. Chan grew more and more peaked; Sister Matty and Mamie could not divine why. By watching they learned of the eating of the kernels. Poor Matty and Mamie! They did the best they could. They were very young. They talked to Chan and explained, but found he was continuing to eat the kernels. Finally they threatened awful things if he ate any more; and then—he was found cracking peach stones!

It was a hot, hot August day. Mamie undressed him and put him to bed. Then she told him he was not to get up till morning, *and was to have no supper!* Chan wept, and we sat at the top of the stairway and wept and wailed. We declared Mamma would never have done that to him. It was too much! Chan was literally drowning his pillow, and we on the top step were keeping pace with him.

Then Chan put the finishing touch. He came to the head of the steps, and whispered, "Fonnie, couldn't you ask Mamie to let me have a teeny, tiny crust of bread, no longer than that?" measuring on his thin little finger. That thin little finger, and Chan's meager, peaked little nightgowned self overwhelmed us. I am sure there was no pleasure in that supper for big or little. Of course, Chan wasn't really hungry, none of us were. We had probably that afternoon eaten all the peaches we could carry. It was only the ignominy of having supper denied him. The next morning the storm had blown over. Mamie was as good to us as ever, and we had forgiven her, but we never forgot it. Fonnie, Chan, and I have talked and laughed that scene through, many a day. I don't remember whether or not it ended the peach-stone habit. Other things just then began to fill our minds.

We were not getting much very good news from Will. The old surgeon had left Richmond. When he went, he said to Mamma, "Don't let anyone probe for that ball. Captain Ward is doing well. Let the ball alone."

She tried, poor Mamma! But the young surgeons insisted, and Will wanted it. The ball was probed for and taken out. After that the news was never as good as it had been. At first, "Will was feeling the exhaustion from the probing"; then: "The weather was so warm, he was feeling the heat." Mamma said he was longing to get away from the city and under the trees at Bladensfield. At last the news grew to be so discouraging that Charley said he would drive to Richmond, find out just how matters stood, and bring us word.

Today, with automobiles and the bridge over the Rappahannock, it is a trip of a few hours, but with a horse it took a long day to drive to Richmond, starting early in the morning and arriving late. Charley was to leave very early. Dick and Pad, the gallant carriage horses, were dead at a brave old age. We only had Bill now. He was getting old, but the Yankees took everyone's horses. It was risky keeping them, even if we had had the money to buy them.

The grown people were going to send everything they could to Will —fresh vegetables, melons, peaches—the best that could be gathered; and we children were going to send flowers picked from our own gardens where we had tended them ourselves—wonderful flowers, painter's brush, sweet alyssum, daily roses, that I know now would not travel from Bladensfield to Warsaw. In the dawn twilight we tied them in nosegays and smelled them, hoping their sweetness would help Brother Will to feel better. Charley drove off with them and the other things in the spring wagon with old Bill.

Charley was only going to stay a day or two, to see how Will was, and to rest old Bill. We didn't expect to hear from him while he was gone. We had grown very patient about not hearing. It would be a week almost before he came back. But in about four days we had a letter. Will was dead.

He was living, though very weak, when Charley arrived late at night. He had taken all of our flowers—they must have been withered stems— and laid them on Will's pillow. Will took in his hand the beautiful peach Mamma gave him, and was told how the girls had sent so many, but he couldn't eat it. Mamma said, "In the morning you can eat it, Will."

In the morning early, as the day broke, he died. Charley was to stay till Will was buried, then he was coming back to us.

We sat very still. We couldn't even cry. It didn't seem possible that we could go on living with Brother Will gone! Something awful had happened that had changed life. I remember how silent everything was. If a rooster crowed in the chicken yard, you heard it all through the house. If the dog barked, it was a shock. I heard Sister Matty say to Silvie as she was giving out supper, "Nothing can ever be the same, Silvie."

And I was sure it never could. In a day or two we saw Charley driving down the road. We stood in the front door watching. He came slowly. Maybe old Bill was tired, or maybe Charley didn't have the heart to drive faster. When he came into the house, all of us went upstairs and sat close together to hear what he had to say. He told us that though he seemed very weak, Will was glad to see him, and had asked after everybody. Charley told us about the watch—so anxious, though sometimes touched with hope —that he, Mamma, and Papa had kept that night; how in the early dawn Will's life had passed peacefully away. He told us about Will's burial, how beautifully the evening sun had cast its long rays across the grass, how Mamma had held up and had followed through everything till Will's body was laid in the ground; then how she had crumpled against Father like something whose strength was gone, and he had taken her away.

Very shortly after that our Mother and Father came home. It was good to have them with us again. Mamma made life feel less strange, though she was dressed in black and was sad. We pressed around her as she sat with Baby Ran and peaked little Chan in her lap. She cried, but she smiled on us. We sat close together, a sad little group, grown people and children, and she told us about Will's last days. Sometimes at night, when he began to lose strength, he would toss around and couldn't sleep. She would say to him, "Try to lie still, Will, and sleep. You can't get well unless you sleep."

"Oh!" he answered more than once, "If I don't get well, those girls will have to go out to teach."

It was Matty, Mamie, and Eddie he was thinking of.

Once after he had grown very weak and everyone was afraid he would die, Mamma said she leaned over to arrange his pillows. Her face must have shown how she was suffering, for he looked up at her and said, "Mamma, you have taught us all the faith we have, but you haven't faith enough to see me die."

Then that last night when he was almost gone, he raised his eyes to hers and said, "I know that my Redeemer liveth, and that in my flesh I shall see God."

She told us how he had loved the fourteenth chapter of the Gospel of St. John, and how she had read over and over to him, "In my Father's house are many mansions—."

As we listened to her, and as we cried and said our prayers and took in the great vision of our Lord Jesus Christ, we fastened our lives on to Will's new life in Heaven, feeling that he had not really gone away from us. So we grew happy again, our hearts thrilled with desire to be like him.

Children, I want you to think of your Uncle Will. He is someone for you to be proud of. Get out his daguerreotype, and see what a noble purpose shows in his face. He had lived but twenty-three years—a boy, you might almost say—yet when he died, his thoughts were all for us—for Mamma, for his sisters, for us little ones, not for himself.

He had always been like that—I am telling you the truth about him, just as he was. All the way through he had done his best—at school, at the University of Virginia where he went as a state student, at Mr. Roy Mason's where he taught and studied law at the same time. Everywhere he was loved and respected—an acknowledged influence for good. Years later, when the University of Virginia was writing about the students who had lost their lives in the War, I walked behind Lucy and Judge T. R. B. Wright, who had been a student at the University with Will, and heard Judge Wright earnestly beg for the privilege of writing a sketch of Will's life. I remember hearing him say that he had loved Will so dearly, and that he thought that the life of any boy who was so warmly loved by other boys and at the same time such a forceful influence for good, should be recorded. Dear Lucy, who admired this beloved brother so greatly and loved him so much that even then she found it hard to speak of him, asked that nothing should be written of him. It seemed to her a kind of profanation. I think she was wrong.

When Will was only nineteen, our Father had to go South on business. He was gone a year. Will came home and took the management of the plantation like a man. He went to the best farmers near him and asked their advice and counseled with them. Old Captain Hutt, whose farm adjoined

Bladensfield, took the greatest interest in him and his work, and loved him dearly. This was just at the time of John Brown's raid. The white people were on the watch and suspicious, but he managed the Negroes well. He had no trouble. They loved him and would do anything for "Mars' Will." He had great success. Everything turned out well that year.

How we loved him! And now he was dead. But he no longer seemed gone from us. We looked to see him again someday, and we tried to do what would please him.

About this time supplies began to be very scarce. There were no sugar or coffee or tea at the stores, no new calicoes or cottons. There were no men to keep the stores, of course, they had all gone to the War, but their wives and daughters kept the storehouses open when they were not at the Soldiers' Aid Society working for the soldiers.

Living so far away, and having such a large family, our Father had always bought supplies wholesale; consequently, we had a good deal of sugar and coffee on hand. Mother very soon began ways of making her supplies last as long as possible. She had rye toasted with just enough coffee to flavor it, to make the coffee hold out. Father planted a big patch of sorghum. All the neighbors were planting it. Mr. Mothershead, near Lyells', got a mill to grind it and boil the juice down to make molasses, and all the crops of sorghum near us were taken to him. Late one evening we went with Father to see the blazing fires and the great boilers full of syrup. It made fine molasses, and Silvie made good gingerbread with it. When all the candy was gone from the stores, we made taffy of sorghum, and after the October nights had become frosty, we used to cut down a sorghum cane, peel off a joint, and chew the pith.

After the day's work was over, we had a habit of walking up the road together. All went—Father, Mother, all the children, and usually the little blacks. "Walking up the road" meant going up the front driveway to the gate opening on the county road—a distance of three quarters of a mile. In summer and early fall there were so many biting insects, ticks, chiggers, and the like in the woods that the grown people wouldn't go into them often. We children, headed by Lucy and Harry, always went. The woods

William N. Ward at twenty-three. "Brother Will" died in Richmond in 1862 of a shot wound inflicted at the Battle of Gaines's Mill.

were too beautiful to be foregone. But when the whole family went together, it was "up the road." That was pretty, too. The broad fields stretched so softly and tranquilly away beyond the evening shadows; the cloud effects were lovely, and the air fresh and good. After the frosts came, we used to love to see the tall sorghum canes waving their tasseled plumes. It was then that we cut them for candy.

How beautiful the skies looked on those evenings—clear and cool, with sometimes a little crescent moon hanging above the woods, or a big bright star shining out on us as we came home!

Through Mamma's care we had not suffered much from the blockade, but the sugar was getting low. Christmas was looming in the distance and we couldn't make the Christmas cake and pudding with sorghum. Mamma's dried cherries thoroughly drenched with brandy would keep us from missing the raisins. We had homemade citron. But sugar! There was nothing we could use in place of that.

People were beginning to run the blockade for supplies. They would cross the Potomac to Maryland, buy what they wanted, and scurry back, unseen. There was a Mr. Mattox who almost made a business of doing it. Charley wanted to go with him to get some sugar.

It was dangerous, of course. Charley would be eighteen in February, old enough to be in the army. Suppose he should be taken prisoner!

"There is no danger!" asserted Charley.

The truth was that a risk was what Charley loved above all things. Mr. Mattox crossed at night in a rowboat to Leonardtown, bought what he wanted, and came back the same night. Charley wanted so much to go, there was no withstanding him. He went twice, and brought back a good supply of sugar, spices, and other things. Mamma and the other grown people were anxious about him, but each time he came back delighted with his trips, especially if he had seen the gunboats and had had to get away from them.

The terrible War was going on, but we did not see the actual fighting. We were "out of the lines." Great battles had been fought, many of them won by our men. We used to get the Richmond papers—the *Whig* and the *Enquirer*—once in a while. Somebody would read the news aloud. All the rest of us would gather around to hear. The lists of the killed and wounded were always read. We would often read the names of friends. Cousin Philip

Lewis was killed. We had heard how old Uncle Bailor, the carriage driver at Lewis Level, had begged to go to look after "Mars' Phil," and had found him sitting in front of his tent, patching his trousers with a piece of a bag. Uncle Bailor cried when he told his mistress of it, but he said Cousin Philip was as gay as a lark. Now he was dead.

We felt thrilled through and through by the accounts of the brave fighting our dear people were doing. We children were always drilling, marching, fighting—the whites as officers in the front rank, the blacks coming behind. When Lewis went to the pasture for the cows, all of us went with him, "marching." The cows were the Yankees, and I am afraid we didn't always drive them as slowly as our Father wanted them driven. How many lovely times we had "marching" the cows up, then sitting on a top rail of the cowpen to watch dear old Aunt Eve milk, while Lewis kept the calves back till it was time for them to have their supper. I can smell the cows' breath now. I can feel the evening breeze blowing us cool after our "march," and see the long lines of sunlight, and the big, red sun going down behind the woods.

There were more and more raids from the Yankees, who behaved very differently from their ways in the first raids, and took everything they could get. Everybody began hiding their silver and valuables of all kinds.

One day when we were having a drowsy time upstairs over lessons, there was the cry, "The Yankees have come!"

Somebody had met them on the Main Road (the county road). There was no drowsiness after that. Everyone jumped. Mamma put the silver in the big freezer, and made Uncle Charles, the gardener, bury it in the cabbage patch. But the freshly dug ground looked suspicious. Two or three of us set to work and hoed the whole patch over. One cabbage was set immediately over the freezer. As it had very little depth of earth, it never grew as the other plants did. That was how we kept account of where the silver was.

Silverware, whatever crops were newly harvested, horses, and cattle were the things most in danger, though at Belleville, the home of the Brockenbroughs, the Yankees helped themselves to the pickles and preserves they found, and spit into the jars they didn't want to prevent their being used.

At Stratford they had rummaged around, scaring old Mrs. Stork almost to death. They found her bonnet in its bandbox and seemed to get a great amount of fun by tossing it about on their bayonets.

She said to them, "What good can destroying my best bonnet do you?"

"Is this old thing your best bonnet?" they jeered. "Mrs. General Lee ought to be ashamed to call such a thing her best bonnet." Because General Lee was born at Stratford, they thought Mrs. Stork must be his wife.

At some places the Yankees took all the clothes they could find, leaving the family with only the clothes they wore. That alarmed my Mother. She made up a little bundle for each one of us containing an entire change of clothes, and made us take our bundles out of doors and hide them for ourselves. After the bundles were hidden, everyone hunted for those of the others to test whether they were well hidden or not. All things considered, we got a good deal of fun out of the coming of the Yankees.

Soon we ceased to fear the Yankee raiders, because no matter how often they came to our neighborhood, they never came to Bladensfield. We children went on hiding our little bundles of clothes; the silver and the best cut glassware stayed hidden except for special occasions, but no Yankees came. People began to consider Bladensfield a safe place to hide, and sometimes we would have several guests at a time—people who for some reason had to pass through the Northern Neck, and who took refuge here.

The many young Maryland men who had come across to join the Southern army had formed the Maryland Line. When one of the Maryland Line had a furlough, he was very apt to come to our part of the country and go across to Leonardtown with the blockade runners. While he waited the blockade runner's time, Bladensfield was a good safe place to stay. In that way it happened that we very often had a Maryland Liner as guest for a night, a couple of nights, or even a week at a time. My poor dear Mother! It was a pleasure to her to do what she could for those soldier boys who were trying to get a glimpse of home.

The Maryland Liners came so often that it seemed quite like old Tappahannock days with young soldiers coming and going. We had a crowd of them at Christmas. Mamma said, "We must do all we can to make them have a good time."

The silver came out of the cabbage patch, the glass out of its hiding. Mamma made a fine fruitcake, having the sugar Charley had run the blockade to get. She used her dried cherries for raisins, and homemade citron.

In those days there was no such thing as granulated sugar. Sugar came either cut in little cubes or in big cones, tall and hard—sugar loaves. The sugar had to be beaten to powder for cake. We children beat it in a little white stone mortar with a white stone pestle, and sifted it through muslin before our Mother thought it right for cakemaking. We had to beat the spice, too. There was no ground spice in those days, either North or South.

Sister Matty always beat the whites of the eggs. She had to beat them till they were so stiff she could hold the dish upside down without the eggs slipping off. Mamma beat the yolks while Silvie creamed the butter. Mamma would have thought melted butter scandalous. Fruitcake was never baked in the stove. The old oven was kept for that. Children: it is still in the pantry. You can go and see it there.

So, trying to make things merry for us children and for the Maryland soldiers, Mamma stilled her heartache this first Christmas without our Brother Will. She had a Christmas tree in the studio trimmed with long strings of hollyberries and lighted by nub ends of candles. We had no presents for the soldiers, so we made them little round pincushions, but put no pins in them. Pins were scarce and precious in those days.

We children had our things in our stockings early in the morning. We cared much more for our stockings than for the tree. We had heaps of things. Each one of us made rag babies for the others. Charley, who could make anything, made "wood-sawyers" for us. We set them on the mantle-piece, and they would saw for hours without stopping. The girls made new dresses for our big dolls. Silvie made us gingerbread men. Mamma had all kinds of little cakes, dried cherries, rolls of peach-leather, handfuls of chestnuts. Long before light, the little servants came to watch us "Chri'mus gif." The boys began firing firecrackers and bursting bladders, and we were out of bed joining in the fun. With Mamma and the girls taking care of them, the soldiers were merry even though their pincushions were without pins. We laughed and talked in spite of the Yankees. I had almost for-

gotten to tell that by some hook or crook, the soldiers managed to get a box
of real candy for the girls.

The winter was passing. Charley would be eighteen in February, old
enough to go to the army. He was still light-hearted and gay, but poor
Mamma! She had to go through all of the old suffering now for him. She
had an idea that being in the cavalry was a trifle safer than the infantry.
Charley loved horses, and could manage them easily. Cousin Waring Lewis,
still captain of his Essex Troop, now a part of the Ninth Virginia Cavalry,
asked to have Charley come to join his company, saying he would gladly do
what he could to take care of him, and it was decided that after his birthday Charley should join Cousin Waring's company.

Charley had a bay colt named "Bedford," a beauty, but terribly wild;
he seemed to prefer walking on his hind legs. All winter long it was our
great interest to watch the training of Bedford. He did his best to throw
Charley, but never succeeded. However, Papa persuaded Charley to part
with him, as in a battle he might be unruly.

When Charley's birthday came, everyone did his best to make it joy-
ful, but I know it must have been sad for Mamma and the grown people.
Charley was gay and bright. He kept everyone laughing at the witty, clever
things he said. He always thought of things just in time. Will used to say
that it was Charley who would be the great lawyer, because he was so
quick and ready. He had seemed a man since he was fourteen. Withal he
was good—never setting his will up against Father or Mother—sweet and
gentle with all of us. Now he too was to go to the War!

Charley was to get a horse in Essex since the Yankees had raked our
country of all that were sound. A short time before he was to leave, he took
a severe cold that brought on a fever and delayed his going. The Yankees
chose that time to come on a big raid. The neighborhood was full of them.
They had never yet come to Bladensfield, but if they should come this time
they would take Charley because he was eighteen. He decided to leave
next morning.

That evening two Southern soldiers rode up. One of them, Captain
Chandler, was a friend from the neighborhood of Oak Grove, a signal

Charles B. Ward at eighteen. "Charley" was a member of the Essex Troop of the 9th Virginia Cavalry and was killed at Beverly's Ford in 1864.

corps officer on duty of observation at the time. The other was a stranger, a young man from Mississippi named Montgomery. They had come to Bladensfield as the safest place to hide, and wanted to leave very early in the morning. We made them welcome. I remember well the supper we had together that evening—anxious, but hopeful. Charley came down, though he still had a fever. He made us laugh with the quick, quizzical things he said.

They were to have breakfast before daybreak, and all three were to leave together. Mamma told the servants they must not open the door in the morning to anyone until Father came down. They were to get up about three o'clock, make the fire in the dining room, and lay the table, but by no means to open the door for anyone.

We children went to sleep, distressed that Charley was to leave, but not much afraid of the coming of the Yankees.

Just as they had been told to do, Louisa and Jack came down about three o'clock, started the fires, and were getting the table ready for breakfast when there came a very soft knock at the south door of the hall. Louisa started toward it, but Jack said, "Don't you remember the mistress said not to open the door to anyone?"

"Pshaw! Boy," said Louisa, "do you think the Yankees would knock like that? That is just Mr. Davis (the overseer) come to say that the horses are ready."

She went softly to the door, intending to peep out. The big back door of the main hall at Bladensfield is a very odd affair. It is made of heavy oak timbers sheathed with the same laid diagonally. It has the old HL hinges "warranted to keep the witches out," and has never had any other fastening than a latch, a bobbin, and a heavy oaken bar across it for security. Cautiously Louisa lifted one end of the bar—Bang! It fell to the floor from a push outside. In a moment the hall was full of Yankees.

Mamma, Papa, every one of us jumped from our sleep at the sound. Louisa came flying upstairs, screaming, "Mars' Charley! Mars' Charley!"

Mamma rushed out without even putting on her slippers. At the landing of the stairway she met a surge of great armed men, wet and cold from the rain outside. She held out her poor helpless arms to keep them back, as frantic Louisa ran to Charley's door to waken him.

Of course, they put Mamma aside as if she were a straw, and followed

The great south door—"In a moment the hall was full of Yankees."

Louisa to Charley's door. He was fast asleep, and drowsy with fever be-sides. He came to the door half aroused.

"Henry David," he said, "is that you?"

"Yes, Charley," the foremost Yankee said. "Strike a light."

"Plague take you," answered Charley cheerfully, "you are Yankees."

He struck a match and lighted a candle as the soldiers pressed into the room, shutting the door behind them.

Outside, Mamma was knocking, demanding, "Let me in! Let me in!" The soldiers took no notice.

"That is my Mother," said Charley. "Let her in."

"You put your clothes on," said the foremost Yankee, who, we later found, was the second officer in command.

But Charley moved to the door and opened it. The officer held a pistol cocked for firing at Charley's breast, warning him not to move. He did not move, but held up his hand and said in the tone of a mother to a naughty child, "Don't play with those things. They are dangerous."

Mamma told us that the Yankee laughed and lowered his pistol. "You are a cool one!" he said.

"Oh! Charley!" Mamma had her arms around him. He took her cold hands in his with a cheering word on his lips, upholding her with his courage.

The whole party of soldiers were so absorbed with taking Charley that the grown people wondered if they knew anything of Captain Chandler and Mr. Montgomery. Papa slipped into their room. They had wakened, but they saw there was no way of escape. Under each of their windows an armed sentinel stood. The only door opened on the main upper hall that was now full of soldiers. Later on, Sister Matty said that as she passed the half-opened door, she saw a Yankee helping Mr. Montgomery into his clothes with great friendliness.

When she ran out, Mamma had not thought of us, but Papa, before he followed, told us to be good children and stay where we were till somebody came for us. We could hear the strange noises about the house. I, for one, was trembling from head to foot. We dressed ourselves. The little servants, Amy, Maria, and Lewis, came down from their rooms and made fire for us. We were all as still as mice, wondering what was going on. Amy looked out of a window. "Oh! Look here!" she cried in a whisper.

We went to the window and saw a Yankee with a gun standing under it, looking straight up at us. We went to all the windows, in Mamma's room, in the nursery, in the little hall, and the closet—all were just the same—a Yankee with a gun under each was looking straight up at us—and the grown people had forgotten us!

We knelt down all at one chair and prayed. For my part, I was crying my eyes out.

When Ran, the baby, awoke, Stell took him carefully out of the crib—he was three years old now, big and heavy—dressed him, and we gathered close around the fire. Outside we heard footsteps, some that we knew, some that were heavy and strange. And Mamma didn't come! We decided to go out. Stell wrapped the baby carefully in Mamma's shawl, for it was chill and damp; she gave him to Lewis to carry, and we went into the hall.

Mamma was packing some clothes for Charley. The hall was full of Yankees, but they seemed to be acting in a very friendly manner. One of them said to Mamie, "Can't you get your Ma to put on some stockings? She really will take cold."

Captain Chandler and Mr. Montgomery were dressed and out among the others. We went to the end of the hall by Charley's room that we might see him and Mamma. Stell and Fonnie went up the garret stairs a little way and leaned over the banister to see more. They began to talk and even to laugh a little, but I was watering the floor with my tears, my apron held up to my eyes.

The commanding officer of the Yankee force was standing opposite Charley's door. He was Captain Wadsworth of a New York regiment; as I remember, it was the Sixth New York. He laid his hand on my head and said in a kind voice, "Sissy, don't cry. We will bring him back again."

Oh! Dreadful! A Yankee soldier had patted me on the head! I felt disgraced, disloyal to Will, to Charley, to my whole world, especially so because in my heart I felt his kindness and felt drawn to him. The children hanging over the garret stairway jeered me. "Hum-m-mm-p! Let a Yankee pet you!" they called. Oh! I was disgraced!

Captain Wadsworth turned to Ran. Lewis was holding him wrapped up in Mamma's shawl.

"What's your name, little fellow?" he asked.

"I'm a Rebel," Ran answered. He had picked that up, and always said it when his name was asked.

"Poor little man!" said Captain Wadsworth. "I hope it will all be over before you are old enough to have anything to do with it."

Uncle Charles came from the stables and said that the Yankees had Captain Chandler's and Mr. Montgomery's horses and our old Bill, and had cut all of the saddles to pieces.

"That horse is a great favorite of mine," Captain Chandler said to Captain Wadsworth. "I would pay high for him."

"I am not to be bribed," answered Captain Wadsworth haughtily.

"That's good, from a Yankee," said Captain Chandler, which I now think was a nasty speech, though it amused us at the time, as did something that Mr. Montgomery said. One of the Yankees came to him as he was talking to Eddie and asked, "Have you any side arms?"

"Yes, Yankee," said Mr. Montgomery, in the very gentle voice he had.

"You must deliver them up," the soldier replied.

Mr. Montgomery felt in the depths of his pocket, brought out an old pocket knife with a broken blade, and passed it over.

"That is no side arm," said the Yankee indignantly.

"That is all I have, Yankee," Mr. Montgomery returned urbanely, and went on talking to Eddie.

It would seem as if this manner of receiving them would have irritated our enemies, but there must have been something of pluck and courage that pleased them instead. The roughness of their manner on entering the house changed to the greatest kindness and consideration from all of the officers. Every one of them addressed Charley as "Charley." They spoke of Mr. Chandler as "the friend of the family," and Mr. Montgomery they called "the courting man." Altogether they seemed to get a deal of interest and entertainment out of our household.

Our Mother tried to induce them to let their prisoners have breakfast before they left, but this was refused. Captain Wadsworth said he must set off as quickly as possible, but he said Mamma could give them something to take with them. They could eat it after they reached the camp. Mamma, Lucy, and Louisa put up a package of lunch. When they brought it upstairs, Captain Chandler said, "Miss Mamie, I know you want me to help you twist a strong string for that lunch."

Mamie, with her quick wit, guessed he had something to tell her. She brought a long, thin string, and she and he twisted it, both talking gaily as they worked. When they came close together to double the string, Captain Chandler said, "Open the mattress of my bed after I'm gone."

They were ready to go now. We went to the door with them. It was raining steadily—bleak, chill March weather. Pale daylight was glimmering. Charley looked out and saw the horses from our stables held in front of the house. "Mamma," he said anxiously, "they have old Bill. You won't have a horse even to send to the mill."

"Never mind, my child," our Mother said. Her arms were around him, her drawn, suffering face held up for his kiss. "Since they are taking you, nothing else matters."

Sister Matty looked at the falling rain and then at the raincoats the Yankee officers wore.

"Oh! Charley," she said, "if you only had a raincoat, as these Yankees have! You with a fever at this minute, and going out in this rain."

Lieutenant Biddle, the second officer in command, promptly took off his raincoat and said, "Here, Charley, put this on."

"Your coat!" said Charley, warding it off. "You are deranged, I know."

"Put it on," said the officer commandingly. "You must do now what I bid you. You have a fever. I am well." He helped to button Charley up in his coat.

"Thank you," said Sister Matty gratefully. "Thank you with all my heart. That is a kind act. More than we could have asked."

They started off in the rain, swords clanking, the pistols in their belts creaking, Charley buttoned up in Lieutenant Biddle's raincoat.

"Ha! Ha!" laughed old Uncle Charles, wagging his head and slapping his legs as he watched them go. "Jes' wait till good daylight shines through ole Bill's ribs! I lay they won't want him any longer."

We felt blank enough with Charley gone off to prison. As he had told her to do, Mamie went upstairs and looked in the mattress of Captain Chandler's bed. It had been ripped up, a package of reports slipped in, and then resewed. I have forgotten how she managed it, but Mamie got the reports to Headquarters. That is how General Lee got his reports that time, though his signal corps officer was taken prisoner.

While we were at breakfast, just as Uncle Charles had said, old Mr. Corns, whose little house was at the corner of our land came bringing old Bill back. He said the Yankees had given the horse to him, and he, recognizing our old nag, had brought him home.

Old Mr. Corns was a Pennsylvania Dutchman who had moved into our neighborhood a few years before the War began. Naturally, he was all for the Yankees. Everyone knew this, though he was afraid to show his real sympathies among such fiery Southerners. He was a good old neighbor and harmed nobody, and nobody wanted to harm him. Charley got an amount of fun out of him. When we had a victory, Charley would go and tell Mr. Corns all about it in the most glowing manner. Mr. Corns would receive the news with a great many exclamations, "Oh!" "You don't say so!" "My! My!," as if delighted. Then, heaving a deep sigh and slowly moving his head from side to side, he would come back with, "But I guess they'll crush us in the end."

I can hear Charley tell that story now. He enjoyed so thoroughly Mr.

Corns' "us!" Now the old man had brought back old Bill to us. He was fond of Charley, for all of his teasing. I like to remember old Mr. Corns' life among us during the War. We were kindly neighbors through it all.

Later in the day the March rain changed to a fitful, chill blur of light. It wasn't pleasant out of doors. We felt strange and dreary wherever we were. We sat in a ring on the floor and picked cotton, though without our usual singing.

One thing appeared strange to us. Phil, the Negro that my Mother and the family generally rated as our most reliable man, did not come to the house till late in the day after the Yankees had taken Charley. When he did come, he was furtive, and different from the rest of our "people," who were natural and warm in their sympathy. Poor Louisa was almost ill from grief because she had opened the door.

Years afterward, a neighbor of ours, Edward Newton, told us that though he was a boy he had been taken into custody by the Yankees and taken to their camp. As he sat on the body of a cart near the campfire waiting to see what disposition was to be made of him, he saw a body of soldiers bring in our Phil and Captain Hutt's John. They were told that they must guide a party to Bladensfield. When they showed reluctance, the officer said if they failed to guide the party faithfully they should have their ears and toes cut off. Edward Newton said Phil seemed almost paralyzed with fright and showed the greatest distress. I have no doubt that he and John did act as guides, but we never blamed Phil or questioned him.

We were glad when the day drew to a close and we sat together around the fire before bed. It seemed an age since the night before.

"Mamma," asked Baby Ran, "if he should push and pull very hard don't you believe that tall, round-headed Yankee who lent Charley his overcoat could get to Heaven?"

"I believe he could, Ran," answered Mamma, holding his baby hand pressed against her face.

We had long stopped using candles or lamps, except for high occasions. Every day that winter Uncle Charles had brought in a big armful of light wood knots split into good sizes and laid them beside the hearth. "Marster's Configity Candles," he called them. One knot at a time laid on the fire would cast a brilliant, ruddy glow to the very back part of the room. It was too flickering a light to read or sew by, but it was grand for talking and knitting.

There was always a great amount of knitting done in our household, chiefly during the winter. All of our under-flannel was knit, and papa's and the Boys' socks and gloves. Mamma's needles flew like the wind. She used a "knitting sheath" made of the wing bone of a turkey enclosed in a flap of cloth by which it was pinned to her side. Her needle was stuck into the hollow bone as a rest. A new knitting sheath for Mamma was always made by us young ones each Christmas. We would save up the turkey bones for that purpose.

We went with Uncle Charles when he got the "Configity" candles. The whole troop of us followed him into the woods in the clear, cold winter light, looking for the lightwood logs or roots of cut-down pine trees. The roots made the best lightwood. While Uncle Charles did his investigation, we scrambled through the woods, sat on fallen logs, looked for cup moss, sage green with red linings. The cup mosses were our fairy cups, and the red lining was the staining of fairy wine. We drank in the pine fragrance, and coming home, watched the clear horizon above the treetops. Maybe, if Uncle Charles was late, a big star would shine out of the clear, opal depths as the world around draped itself in twilight.

As the pine knots were not much good for reading, Sister Matty told us stories—whole novels that took nights and nights in the telling. I remember she told us *Zaudee, Lena Rivers,* and *Mabel Vaughan,* while Mamma, Mamie, Eddie, and Lucy knit, and Papa made his axe halves glossy smooth with bits of broken glass, and also new knitting needles for the girls.

Father used to make shot and bullets. He wrapped slugs of lead in wads of wet paper, and heated clamps (sometimes the ends of the fire tongs) red hot. Then he took up the lead with the clamps, having punched round holes in the wet papers, and held it over a pan of cold water. In a few minutes the melted lead would drop down into the water, making very fair shot. He made bullets on the same principle, the size of the holes in the wet paper making the size of the bullets.

***

With Charley in prison, we could not go back to our winter ways. Mamma said that at least he was not always in danger of being shot. Sometimes prisoners were exchanged, and he might soon come back to us, though the North with its ready supply of fresh troops was not very keen on exchange.

The spring came on beautifully. Ice wreaths on the sides of the brooks were melting away and arbutus buds were peeping up on the hillsides. Wrens in the garden sang all day long. Johnny-jump-ups were blooming on the edges of the walk. Anyone had to be rather happy with everything calling and the sun shining so wondrously, Uncle Charles spading up the flower borders, and Phil with old Bill turning up the sweet-smelling earth in the vegetable squares.

After lessons were done, the white children worked with the blacks, picking up dead weeds and trash and piling them in great piles. We had always loved to watch them burn at night. We just stood and watched the burning, because Harry didn't have the heart to run and jump through the blaze with no Charley there. He had been the heart and the life of everything.

Lucy and Harry went with us into the woods where the brown hillsides were warm in the sun. We caught minnows and mellow bugs, and gathered the yellow spicewood blooms and the red maple keys. Harry made us chestnut whistles all around. He did his best, but how we missed Charley! And longed for him in his prison. We had hard thoughts of the Yankees who kept him there. I might have learned my music better if, while I played my scales up and down, I had not thought but how when next I saw the Yankees I would not cry, but would stand up and tell them how bad they were. One day, while I was busy doing this, Fonnie came sidling into the parlor and whispered, "There's a Yankee in the yard. He has been to the kitchen and now he is on his way to the house."

I jumped up. I did not feel half as brave as I had done the minute before. Fonnie and I thought we would find Mamma. As we came into the hall, we saw the Yankee at the door. He had a drawn sword in his hand and looked very much as if he would cut us. "Where is your Father?" he asked fiercely.

I answered meekly, "I don't know, sir," and Fonnie slid down to the floor.

He passed on to the dining room where the grown people received him with much laughing. He wasn't a Yankee at all—only Mamie dressed in Papa's Virginia soldier clothes, her hair knotted high up under his hat, her father's sword in her hand. The first person she had spoken to was Silvie who was in the turnip patch gathering turnip greens for dinner. Silvie hadn't thought a minute. She threw her knife at the "Yankee" and came running to the house.

I think it was in May that we got a newspaper from somewhere and read of an exchange of prisoners. Charley might be among them. We hoped, and feared to hope. Sister Matty read that as the Confederate prisoners were marched down Pennsylvania Avenue, one of them threw up his cap and shouted, "Hurrah for President Davis!"

"It would be just like Charley to do that," she said.

Some days went by. We looked for Charley all the time. At last one of our kind neighbors drove up in his little spring wagon, bringing him back. I remember how bright the spring sunshine was, and how we went swarming out to the wagon, so thankful and glad to get Charley back from prison.

When he first came, he seemed his old joyous self, but we noticed that soon he settled down in a quiet way, not exactly as if he were thinking, more like dreaming. Mamma asked, "What are you thinking about, Charley?"

He came back like someone waked up. "It is sitting so long in that prison with nothing to do," he said. "It was like being dead."

I don't remember whether Mr. Montgomery came back with Charley, or very soon after he got home. At any rate, he was at Bladensfield while Charley was with us. He told us it was Charley who hurrahed for President Davis as he came down Pennsylvania Avenue.

"Why did you do that, Charley?" Mamma said, smoothing his hair. "They might have put you back again."

Charley laughed. "I thought it a good plan to let them hear a first-rate Southern cheer," he said. "I didn't think they would put me back for that."

Mr. Montgomery told us of some hard experiences that Charley had passed through. He had been put to sleep in blankets in which a poor prisoner had just died of smallpox. Charley had been well vaccinated, but he took a severe case of varioloid. He was very ill, his head so affected by fever that he did not know what he was doing or saying. For fear of the prisoners escaping, the law of the prison was that whoever leaned against the windows was to be shot. Mr. Montgomery said when Charley did not know where he was or what he was doing and the prison air was so bad, he was always trying to go to the window. Mr. Montgomery was so anxious about him because one young prisoner was shot while he and Charley were there. It happened that the mother of the boy who was shot had obtained permission to go to see her son. She reached the prison—the Old Capitol Prison in Washington—a few minutes after her boy had been shot. He was still lying dead on the prison floor.

The Old Capitol Prison was only two or three tall gray dwelling houses overlooking East Capitol Square. This terrible law might have been made because escape would be so easy. When I was in Washington after the War was over, the old building was used as a boarding house.

Charley told us about a little boy, eight years old, who was in the prison all the time that he, Charley, was there. The little fellow was the son of an army officer (or of a naval officer, I have forgotten which) who had resigned and gone South. The officer did not succeed in getting his family off when he left. His little son was held as a hostage for his father's return. Charley said the mother of the boy came every day or so to see him. She had a Confederate captain's uniform made for him, which he wore. The prisoners called him "Captain" and made a great pet of him.

Charley told us that Captain Wadsworth and Lieutenant Biddle were good to him all the time he was with them, but he said they did not behave well when they went into other Southern homes, as they had done in ours. Once, when they went into a very poor home and broke up things, Charley said he asked Captain Wadsworth how he could bring himself to do it. The Captain answered that that was one way of winning the War.

Charley stayed with us about two weeks before going off to the front. I remember the lilies were in bloom when he left. The evening before he went, we sat around the south door of the hall, all of us together. I remember the smell of the lilies, and how they gleamed in the twilight. The stars looked down on us through the misty branches of the mimosa trees. Everyone tried to be cheerful, but it was hard.

In the morning he rode off on his beautiful chestnut sorrel, Senator. Senator could go as swiftly as Bedford did, but he was gentle and obedient. Father had tried hard to find a suitable mount for Charley, and he had succeeded. Charley went to join the Essex Troop in the Ninth Virginia Cavalry with Cousin Waring Lewis as captain. Cousin Waring had written Mamma that he would do all he could to take care of Charley, and we knew he would.

We followed our soldier to the circle, saying our good-byes, and then stood watching as long as we could see him. At the lawn gate he looked back to wave to us. He was manly and cheerful, but it was not our gay Charley who disappeared under the cedars.

Well, the days went by. We were more used to war by this time. It was only Mamma who never could get used to it in the least. We thought about Charley and prayed that he might come back to us, but we lived and enjoyed the beautiful June weather. I remember it was a very, very warm June. We little ones took off our shoes and stockings. We dearly loved to do it. It was such freedom. Now we could always paddle in the stream or after the rain, in the mud puddles, without even asking permission. Yes, we enjoyed our lives, though our dear Charley was at the front.

One day—it was the ninth of June—we had had our lessons in the morning and a long afternoon of play. When the shadows were long, and the evening breezes had cooled the earth, we little ones, whites and blacks, played Fox and Geese and Puss Wants a Corner on the circle, and Dick's Land across the road till we were called in for prayers and bed. Such a warm night! Every window in the old house was wide open. We lay on our beds without even a sheet over us, and slept—such good sleep—until in the early morning when the newly risen sun was slanting long rays across the grass, there came such a cry—if I live to be a hundred years old, I shall never forget it—such a cry of agony sounding through the rooms! It was our Mother's voice. We sprang from our beds. No one told us what had happened. We didn't need to be told. We saw our Mother standing with a bit of a note hanging limply from her poor distraught hands. Papa and the older girls were trying to comfort her. I don't think she heard what they said. I can never forget her tearless face.

Outside a horse was fastened on the circle road, and a Negro man stood by it. It was this man who had brought the note from Belleville. Mrs.

Brockenbrough had heard by some means that there had been a battle—a mere skirmish—at Beverly's Ford, near Rapidan. Only a few were killed, but our Charley was among the few. Kind Mrs. Brockenbrough wrote that someone—some of our friends—had seen him propped up against a tree after he had been shot—our Charley! Barely eighteen, shot in his own Virginia fields.

I remember the beautiful June days that passed after that morning. They seem dim and sad to me. For days our Mother stayed in her room like an ill person. She was ill—ill from her heart. It seemed as if she couldn't stand up under this second blow. The grown girls did what they could and took care of the house and children.

Sometimes one or another of us would tiptoe into her darkened room, take her a flower, or just stand by her. I remember her face of tearless suffering. She would speak to us, hold our hands in hers, but it seemed as though she could not move or live.

Father went off immediately to find our Charley's body. One lovely evening, when the long lines of light were sloping to sunset, he came back bringing Senator. We went to the foot of the circle to meet them, the girls trying to give a cheerful welcome, though tears were close. Senator put down his head to our pats, rubbing us with his soft nose, giving us his low, throaty greetings.

We went up to Mother's room. She had thrown back the blinds to let in the sweet evening. Our Father, sitting by her side, told of the simple funeral at Hollywood and what Cousin Waring had told him of Charley.

The Essex Troop, or the whole Ninth Cavalry, I don't know which, had been cut off from the rest of the army. Some of the troopers were detailed to hold the horses while the others cut a way through the Northern ranks. I don't understand this; I only tell it as I remember it. Recalling his promise to Mamma to look out for him, Cousin Waring appointed Charley among the number to hold the horses. One of the men detailed to go said it was not fair. "I have a wife and children dependent on me at home," he said. "Ward is a mere boy. No one is dependent on him."

Before Cousin Waring could speak, Charley said, "He is right, Waring. I ought to go, and he to stay. It is my place to go." He was steadfast. Cousin Waring knew he was right, and named him to go.

The tears rained down our Mother's face as she listened to this story of the fineness and nobility of her brave boy. It seemed to soothe her poor, tortured heart. She came down to supper with us that evening. So we took up our life again with our gay Charley gone, except from our hearts and our hopes, where we hold him always.

About this time I began to wake up to the power that Eddie's music was in our household. She had a habit in the morning, directly after breakfast, of flooding the house with her grand chords. The door of the parlor where the piano was would be open. Her music went everywhere, calling, compelling, quieting, uplifting. In the evening twilight, even in the darkness, when there were no lights because it was too warm and because they brought in the little bug friends through the unscreened windows, her strong, supple white fingers could find the keys as by magic. Grown people and children loved to sit around the south door of the hall where the breeze always came and where the mimosas had closed their fernlike leaves to make only a soft mist through which the stars looked. Then Eddie's evening music would come to us, soft, clear, appealing, speaking to us of so many things.

One day in the late summer of 1864, Stell, bringing an old blue-backed blank book and the nib of a lead pencil, came out as we were playing. Papa had been cleaning out his papers and had given these to Stell. "I am going to write a story in it," Stell said.

I wondered I had never thought of that before. I didn't write too well, and I spelled worse, but what did that matter! I could make up all the people I wanted, and have them be and do just what I liked! It would be even better than rag dolls.

Mamma did not approve of writing stories, but she did not forbid doing it. Mamie had done a lot of it. Lucy had read some of her stories and said they were as good as those she read in *Godey's Lady's Book*, and better, but Mamma did not like us to read the *Godey's Lady's Book* stories. Mamie kept her writings hidden upstairs. However, we were not forbidden to write, and we felt as if we had to do it. I went to Papa to see if he hadn't another blank book to give me. He hunted around till he found a little paperbacked one—not a grand book with boards like Stell's—and he lent me his own pencil. Blank books and pencils were scarce and hard to get in those days.

"Don't lose it, Shevie," he said. "It is the only one I have."

I promised. We took our books and pencils down into the orchard, climbed one of the dear old cheese apple trees and began to write. What a glorious time we had! I wondered we had never done it before. Things to write just flowed into our minds.

I can see those two books now. I love them yet. Stell's was about six inches square—light blue with cream-colored skin edges. It wasn't altogether blank. Some of its pages had such entries as: Married at such and such a place, So and So, Whites, and very often it was "Negroes," for our Father was a favorite with both "Po' Whites" and Negroes. They often asked him to marry them. Then again, the entries would be: Baptized on such a date in such a place. So and So. My book had such entries as: 186–, so many bushels of corn from the Big Field, or "from the meadow field," maybe, or: So many bushels of potatoes. We didn't mind the entries. We wrote up to every entry, then skipped and began below.

Stell and I evidently were moved by different literary motifs. I ran to short, exciting stories, she to the sustained novel. Her story had many characters. There was a large family of beautiful daughters. Each one had a lover. I had a lone heroine that I put through all manner of nerve-wracking experiences. I named her "Barcelona." I had learned that name in my geography a few days before. It seemed to me the name had an open-hearted, generous sound. My heroine looked like the young lady in one of the fashion plates of *Godey's Lady's Book*. She wore a big hoop skirt and a blue silk dress with large lace undersleeves. I know now that some of her characteristics were those of Mamie.

What we wrote we read to each other. We had a beautiful time, Stell and I. I hope I did not lose Papa's pencil, but I am afraid I did. We hid our stories like lynxes. I don't know why, but it seemed to us that to have anyone see them would be like death.

Fonnie had no part in these hidden delights, perhaps because she was so young, but I rather think it was because even then she was living with that big-hearted interest and intensity in the real life around her that has

CONFEDERATE STATES OF AMERICA, WAR DEP'T,

Richmond, *April 9* 1864.

Pass

to

Subject to the discretion of the Military authorities.

Provost Marshal.

DESCRIPTION.—Age *57*, Height *6·4* Eyes

Hair

charged her whole life. Idle imaginings had no place with her yet. She and I wrote together later, but it was after Life had taught her. Her keen eyes saw many things that passed me. She was sport for the Boys' teasing, never "took a dare," and was full of gaiety and fun.

One bad, drizzly day in December, 1864, as the finishing touches were being given to some job in the Long Room, and I was reveling in *Grace Leigh,* somebody called out, "Here comes Papa, and he has soldiers with him."

We ran to the window to watch Papa drive around the circle through the rain, in the old buggy, two soldiers on horseback following him. That was exciting. We hurried downstairs to hear the news.

The soldiers were Mosby's men. General Lee had had a detachment of Mosby's Raiders sent to our neighborhood to keep off raiding parties of the Federals who came so frequently to take off any crop of food or forage to be had. The men were to be quartered with the households for a small remuneration, the two who came with Papa being our quota. Our two soldiers were Mr. Whiting and Mr. Otho Butler. Mr. Whiting was a nice-looking, quiet young fellow; Mr. Butler a long, tallow candle of a boy hardly grown.

The next day was Sunday. Our soldier boys rode behind the omnibus that took us to church. As we passed a neighbor's gate, another young soldier was pacing up and down. He had an anxious, worried face. Mr. Butler checked his horse and talked to him, then trotted to the window of the omnibus and told Sister Matty that the soldier at the gate felt unsettled at his lodging place, for what reason I don't know. "I told him," said Mr. Butler, "to come to your house. Maybe you could take him in. I know he would like living at your house."

After being at church so long with only women, except for Mr. Fisher and our Father, the two clergymen, it seemed strange to see so many soldiers. Every household brought its quota. There was a rattle of pistol holsters and sabers when the soldiers knelt or rose up, for they came fully armed and ready for a sudden attack.

When we got home, we found the little soldier we had passed on the road. He was Alec Carey from Baltimore, a lovable, dear young fellow. Our Mother had him already installed. This was how a friend—a family of friends—came into our life who were never to leave it.

I don't remember just how it happened, but soon our house was overflowing with soldiers. From two, our quota rose to four. We had two large rooms we could give them, with two double beds in each. The soldiers—most of them hardly more than boys, who had made friends with each other like schoolmates—gave us to know they did not object to crowding so long as they could select their crowd. Mr. Butler went off on a furlough. His place was promptly filled by someone else. As like seeks like and as school boys and girls settle to their own levels, our soldiers soon settled themselves to a pleasant comradeship. Our Father and Mother knew the families of almost everyone who finally lived with us. This added to the easy sociability of our winter together.

Besides our regular inmates, there was a constant influx of visiting soldiers from neighboring houses—sometimes from households where soldiers were not made as much at home as our dear Mother had to make all of them at ours.

Every soldier kept a horse—many of them, two. Alec Carey kept two—Paul, a little sorrel, and Angel, a rather mangy-looking gray. Alec, being a city boy, did not know much about taking care of horses. Boyd Smith, a boy from Alexandria, was one of our visiting soldiers. He seemed always at our house. He had two horses—Dandy Devil and Nigger Baby. Dandy Devil was a shiny bay, and Nigger Baby a coal black. Boyd was a city boy, too, but you could almost see your face in the hides of both of his horses. They were beauties; the kind of horses that do not like to stand on all four feet at the same time when they have to stand, and that go like the wind when they are allowed to go.

Chan was six years old now. He loved the outdoors and to be around with the horses and animals generally. He was a stout little fellow with round rosy cheeks, and courage enough to tackle anything. He rode every horse that came to our house that winter. The soldiers provided the feed for their horses and took care of them. They were glad enough to have Chan ride them down to water, at the stream, a good quarter of a mile from the stables. Down such a hill, too! It scares me now to think of that little fellow riding those fiery horses down that steep, broken road, but he held on and loved it.

Boyd Smith loved to ride Dandy Devil and Nigger Baby up where our girls could see him. The more the horses pranced and went on their hind legs, the more he liked it. He was just nineteen. His forehead was like a snowbank. I never saw such a complexion except on a girl's face. His hair was a mass of golden rings, his lips a soft, fresh rose red, and his blue eyes full of mischief of every kind. Dear Stell! She admired him so much that I accused her of being in love with him and made her weep bitter tears as she denied it. Stell was thirteen now, but she was tall and looked fifteen. She was clever, quick, and handsome, and the young men began to treat her like a grownup. She loved Boyd Smith's pranks. All of us liked to be around when he was in the parlor. We were sure of a good laugh, though what he did does not seem so very amusing to me now. After I was a grown woman, I met Mr. Smith in Washington. His hair was gray, his color was gone. He was just a man like other men. I hope Heaven, somewhere, keeps for us all those radiant creatures we knew when they were young.

Mr. Dennis was my favorite. He was small and dark, not particularly handsome, but he had a beautiful voice and sang a great many songs—some beautiful, some comic. Sometimes he said such funny things, he kept everyone laughing. Sometimes he was moody and silent—wouldn't say anything, but I kept close to him. I knew he would come out of that mood. He was very sensitive because he was so small. Once he told Sister Matty, "I never can feel like a real man among those tall fellows." If anyone "made small" of him, he went into his shell like a turtle. He drew the funniest pictures, and because I was so faithful to him, he used to give them to me. He read a great deal. When the weather was good, which it often was that winter, he would take me out with him and read poetry to me—Wordsworth and Tennyson; sometimes I could and sometimes I couldn't understand it, but I always loved the rhythmic sounds and I dearly loved to have him want to read to me. I was only eleven. I could love anybody as much as I liked. I rubbed his spurs and kept them bright for him. He was a lazy soul. He had one poor horse and he didn't halfway attend to that. When the spring came on, I picked great bunches of violets for him to give Sister Matty, to whom he was paying a kind of boyish attention.

It was a gay, pleasant time. Everybody's corn stayed in the corn house and the wheat in the granary. The Yankees never came once that winter. The Mosbyites took some liberties. They never deigned to follow a road. The shortest cut was always their way. When they had been off looking for forage for their horses, we would see them come flying back through any field and over the fences like birds. Sometimes they had Ran, the three-year-old, up in front of them.

Clothes were getting terribly scarce by that time. Nobody could buy any, but we grew cotton and raised sheep. Mamma was very clever at planning materials that little Mrs. Bartlett wove for her. Upstairs, I keep a little roll of the stuffs that they made for us, the little girls. In the corner of the dining-room fireplace stayed a big pumpkin in which wool was dyed red to make the black- and red-striped goods for Ran's first trousers. The pumpkin was supposed to help make the red dye (pokeberries) permanent. Ran was wearing the trousers when the Mosby men came to live with us, and pretty little suits they were. But a hat or cap was beyond Mamma's ingenuity, so she knitted a snug hood for him. He looked rather odd in trousers and a girl's hood, but it was the best that could be done. We didn't bother about small things in those days.

Sometime during the winter, Cousin Norman Randolph joined Mosby's men and came to stay at our house. As he was Cousin Joe Randolph's child and Cousin Joe had always been our Father's intimate friend, Cousin Norman was given almost the place of a son in our household. He held it always. His whole heart seemed to come out to us and I am sure ours did to him. He showed even then the qualities of a leader, and in no time he had the hearts of all the soldiers in our house. Especially Mr. Dennis was devoted to him, perhaps because the two were so different. Cousin Norman's size, strength, and manliness captivated the smaller and weaker, though more brilliant man.

Although he was the gayest of the gay with them, I think a strong factor of Cousin Norman's popularity was the respect his comrades felt for him. It came natural to trust him. He was a Roman Catholic, and very devout. When Ash Wednesday came, he kept an absolute fast; he did not taste a morsel of food all day. Among our young fellows, many were careless; some, I am afraid, really Godless, but there was not one jeering—even joking—comment made. Cousin Norman's religion was too real—not obtrusive, not sentimental—it seemed just to be the principle of life with him.

Cousin Norman was just eighteen when he came to us. A handsome man always, he was a splendid-looking youth. Six feet or over, well-developed and sinewy, he carried himself as straight as his Pocahontas blood warranted. Geranium red bloomed up in his smooth brown cheeks and in the narrow line of his lips. His hair was silky black, cut close, but duck-tailing at the ends. I know Richmond has not forgotten either him or his wife or their courageous citizenship in the dark days that followed the War.

I used to hear my Father tell of Cousin Joe's aversion to horses. He had had good cause. Cousin Joe's father had been a rich man, living at Warwick, a fine country place near Richmond, but his devotion to horse raising and horse racing had swamped everything by the time his son was a man. I have heard my Mother say that Cousin Joe's father once took his wife and daughters to the races in a fine carriage drawn by thoroughbred horses, bet both carriage and horses away, and came home in a hired hack. I don't vouch for the story, but when I knew of Cousin Joe, Warwick had been sold, and he was making a good living and being a good citizen as a partner in the book-publishing concern, Randolph and English, Publishers.

His two sons, however, suffered from reversion to type. They were devoted to horses. Tucker, the elder, had been shot soon after he went into the War. Norman, though under age, enlisted immediately on his brother's death. He had been in service some time when he came to us, though barely eighteen then. He arrived at Bladensfield with his own horse, Pryor, and Tucker's horse, Mad Sally, both tall sorrels. On her own account, and because she had been Tucker's, Mad Sally was Cousin Norman's beloved. She covered the ground like the wind, but long before you saw her you could hear her blowing as she strained on the bit.

With him Cousin Norman brought a Richmond boy, a friend of his whom he called "Zeke" Shepherd (I think his name was William), a mild-eyed, nervous boy, inordinately devoted to his friend. Everybody liked Zeke too, and made him at home. He was nervously afraid of cats—couldn't stay in the room with one. Our baby, Ran, used to chase him from room to room with our harmless old puss. Sometimes Mr. Shepherd would come down in the morning dumb with doleful dumps. Cousin Norman had hurt his feelings. One day, Mamma said, "Norman, try not to hurt his feelings. He is so devoted to you."

"I know it, Cousin Mary," he answered. "I like the boy too, but I can't have him hugging me at night."

When they were got together in the evenings, what singers our Mosby's men were! Some had fine voices, some couldn't carry the tune. Cousin Norman had a funny little squeak of a voice, but such a dear, bright face that added life to the concert. All sang together—voice or no voice—funny old songs. We learned them every one. "The Yellow Rose of Texas," "Lugianna Quirl," books full of them—some comic, some pretty and pathetic. We left several of the books in the old secretary when we went to stay in Washington; when we came back, the tenants had taken every one.

One day there were a greater number of soldiers than usual to supper. The silver was dug up out of the garden, and the squat cut-glass pitcher (you can see it still in the sideboard, children, if you care to look at it; it has a piece nipped out of the edge now that has been put back by rivets, but it is still pretty) was brought from its hiding place. The long table was full and we children had to sit at the side table. Louisa, Jack, and Lewis were all kept busy waiting on everyone. We were as still as mice at our table so as to hear what was said at the long table; Mamma didn't stand bad or noisy

"Zeke" Shepherd and Cousin Norman Randolph in their Confederate uniforms.

children. The soldiers seemed in a particular merry mood, perhaps because the weather was bad—rain, some snow, and a hard wind—and it was a good evening to be in the house with a big fire blazing up the chimney.

Then all of a sudden—Crash! Bang! Such a noise! It sounded as if every Yankee in the whole Northern army was battering on our house. Everybody jumped up. The soldiers ran into the big hall for their swords and pistols. They weren't hiding. They were Mosby's Raiders and were not to be taken without a fight. There was quite a sound as so many men buckled on their sword belts and pistol holsters, but nothing more was heard from outside except the rushing and sobbing of the wind. Jack peeped through the dining room window. "La! Miss Mary," he whispered, "'tain't nothin' but the tree blowed down."

That was what it was! Just the big ailanthus tree in front of the little-hall back door. It was a very large tree, and had fallen across the doorway and across the whole of that end of the house. You should have heard the laugh that went up from everybody. It was a wonder the house was not injured, but it was not. All of the men went out to see what could be done. They could get out of the south-end door of the big hall. The hall door was completely blocked. We wanted to go out very much, but Mamma said there was too much cold rain. Soon we heard Uncle Charles and Phil hacking away outside. They had to ease up the pressure on the house.

The soldiers came back to supper, in even gayer humor than before; it was a relief not to have a fight on hand and to be again sitting comfortably around the table. After supper there was the smoke by the fire and the air was blue. Each soldier called up some unexpected fight he had been in and told the story of it. We sat among them near our favorites. I was close up by Mr. Dennis. They told of a fight in Winchester where one of them—a mere boy—had been taken prisoner after some daring act. They told with deep drawn breaths how he had been fastened to the heels of an unbroken colt and driven over the rough stones till his brains were dashed out, his mother running behind him in her agony. When he was dead, she was found to be frantically insane. I would like to think they had exaggerated— that it was not just as they told the story. How cruel war can make people. I remember my Mother's hands pressed together and the suffering of her face, yet a certain relief. At least hers could not be put through that!

Then they told of some of Mosby's daring deeds. They told how he had been separated from his men, and had to ride alone through the enemy's sentry line. Suddenly he rode up on one of the sentinels.

"Halt," called the picket, covering Mosby with his pistol.

"Halt, yourself," whispered Mosby. "This is John S. Mosby. If you speak aloud, you are a dead man. Give me that pistol and climb up behind me on my horse, and you shall be saved."

The soldier did as he was bidden. No doubt he thought Mosby had a hidden force around him. Mosby helped him up behind him and rode softly off through the woods. By daybreak, he came back to his own men, bringing his prisoner.

They talked about Philip Stringfellow, or perhaps it was about Bob— I don't remember which of those famous scout brothers it was. Major Richards told the story this time.

"Here come along old Phil, er bobbing and er bouncing like er injur rubber ball. You fellows know how he walks.

" 'Who'll go into the camp and find out what I want to know?' asked the Colonel.

" 'I'm your man,' answered Phil.

" 'You most likely won't come back,' says Mosby.

" 'Maybe I won't; and then again, maybe I will,' says Phil, grinning. 'And I'm betting I will.'

"Well, after he knew just what Mosby wanted to find out, he went. I saw him ride out of camp and down into the woods in the dusk. The moon was just a little mo' than full that night, and it was beautifully clear. Phil had got hold of a Yankee uniform. He hid his horse in the woods, changed his clothes, and then just as it was getting really dark and was time for the moon to rise he come walking boldly into camp. He waited around, keeping in the shadow, watching. Presently he saw a group of officers sitting under a tree, smoking. They had had their supper. Phil walked along keerless-like and lay down in the shadow of the tree trunk. The moon had begun to shine then.

"Bless to goodness if those officers didn't talk over among themselves the very things that Mosby wanted to know. Phil got it all down fine. He lay there till those officers went off to bed, then he backed down the hill in the shadow of the tree trunk. The shadow changed somewhat while Phil was lying there, but he changed with it. He crept down into the gully where he had his horse hidden, got on him, and just skeedaddled back to Mosby. He was a scout, Phil was!"

Then Mr. Dennis got the floor and began to tell of a sharp little skirmish that had taken in most of the fellows around the fire. "You remember how old Turner came charging 'cross country like mad?" said Mr. Dennis. "Half a dozen of us couldn't keep up with him. When we came up out of the woods, not a soul was in sight except an old woman standing over four or five barrels turned over, smashed and mixed up with ashes. Poor old woman! She had her hands up in horror. We asked, 'Have you seen Lieutenant Turner pass here?'

" 'Has I seen him? 'Deed I has seen him. He's jus' now made a streak o' light 'cross my yard, an' knocked down every one uv my lye hoppers!' "

Lieutenant Turner went to the fireplace, beat out his pipe, and re-loaded. "Come, now," he said. "No lies on me." He was blushing scarlet, for all of our girls were listening.

"No lies. Gospel truth." Mr. Dennis welcomed him back by a sounding whack on his leg. "You know how we say, 'Look out when old Turn bursts out crying, and claps his hat under his arm.' We look out for fighting then."

"That's so!" "That's true!" "That's the way he does!" went up a chorus. Lieutenant Turner was completely bowled out.

Here Mamma said, "Look at these children! Go to bed, every one of you."

We hated it, but we had to go. Upstairs, we told it all over to Louisa as she sat on the rug before the fire with all of us piled up on her.

The winter was going. Pleasant, mild days began in February. In that month came James Carey, "Mr. Big Carey," Alec's older brother. One rainy day, a little before suppertime, he appeared. He was a mature man, verging on toward thirty years old, a Baltimorean exquisite in manners and appear-ance. He must have felt like a fish out of water among our rowdy Mosby's Boys. However, he had been roughing and starving with General Hood for some time, and was thankful to get comfortable quarters anywhere.

Mr. Big Carey was one of those enthusiastic Baltimoreans who had rushed out of their places of business and had torn up the street cobblestones to pelt the Massachusetts soldiers marching through their city on their way South. After that he came South himself, and had served under General Hood. Mr. Carey was modest and well mannered and talked but little of himself, but Alec told us of the hard times he had been through. After the War, Mr. Big Carey became our brother-in-law, a good, kind brother-in-law, too, but no one ever ousted our little warfaring Alec from our affections.

He had perfectly lovely peacetime manners, and was shocked when Alec and some others of the Mosbyites raided the Long Room for dried fruits, cherries packed in brandy, nuts, preserves, and other supplies de-sirable to hungry boys between meals. Mr. Big Carey caught Alec red-handed, coming down with his hands full. "Why, Alec," his brother said. "I am surprised at you! You would not have done that in your own Mother's house."

Alec, caught, having nothing to say for himself, looked up with that wistful expression that made his face so lovable, and said nothing. Dear Alec! When we told Mamma, she said Mr. Carey was right. She was much obliged to him for trying to control the younger men. Indeed, all along Mamma had fussed about their lawlessness and complained that she "could not stand such behavior"; yet it seemed to us that she never really tried to put a stop to it. I think she felt so pitiful about their young lives lived in danger that she could deny them nothing.

We felt very shy of Mr. Carey. On a certain hour, some time before dinner, I had to practice my music lesson. One day when I went to this duty, I found Mr. Big Carey ensconced on the sofa reading. Practice before Mr. Big Carey! I couldn't! I waited to see if he would go out, but though the time went slipping, there he sat, as if for a morning's stay. Mr. Dennis was in Papa's big chair in the hall, drawing. I went to him. "Mr. Dennis," I pleaded, "couldn't you get Mr. Big Carey out of the parlor? I must practice, and I can't before him."

Mr. Dennis went on drawing, cruelly, without saying a word.

"Please, Mr. Dennis," I begged.

At last he said, "If you will get me four big ginger cakes, I will get him out."

Four! And Mamma had said she had given them that noon all she could afford, and we mustn't ask for any more. But I got the cakes—I don't remember how. I know I didn't disobediently take them. Perhaps Mamma gave them to me because they were for Mr. Dennis, who was one of her prime favorites.

I came joyfully into the hall and Mr. Dennis went with me into the parlor. "Mr. Carey," he said, "do you know that this young lady has to practice her music lesson, and the fear of doing it before you is about to be the death of her?"

Told him right out that I was afraid to practice before him! These were not the tactics I had expected, but anything was better than having him there.

Mr. Carey looked up from his book and beamed on me with a kind, gentle look peculiar to him. "Little girl, you are not afraid of me, are you?"

Oh! I was—horribly. Like a little country jake, I hung down my head and had not a word to say, though he tried for several minutes to make friends with me. Then he took his book and went into the studio. I went joyfully to my practicing, and Mr. Dennis crunched his cakes and drew pictures.

That year, March was warm and pleasant. The garden borders were white with violets, purple with heart's-ease. I spent myself picking great bunches of them for Mr. Dennis to give Sister Matty. Cousin Norman went home to Richmond on furlough.

Early one morning, a Mosby's man rode in to tell our soldiers the Yankees were landing from the Potomac somewhere in Westmoreland County. All of Mosby's men were to meet at a certain place and go to drive the Yankees back. Our men got ready as quickly as they could. One of them had to ride over to Mr. Porter's farm to tell the soldiers there. Mamma gave our contingent a good breakfast, and they were soon riding across the field. A fight was expected, and Mamma, nervous and distressed, was having something cooked that she could send down to them for dinner when our Maryland Line friend, Mr. Salathiel Cole, rode up. He was on his way to hide around at home on a day or two of furlough, but hearing of the expected fight, determined to cast in his lot with Mosby's men. Mamma made sandwiches of a cold ham she had on hand, boiled a number of eggs, buttered biscuit, and started Mr. Cole off to look for the soldiers.

All day we waited anxiously without hearing a word of news. Late that evening, after dark, a soldier rode up with Colonel Chapman's beautiful horse. It had been badly wounded. Colonel Chapman sent the horse, asking us to hide it in our woods for him. The soldier told us there had been a fight near Kinsale in Westmoreland County. Either Colonel or Captain Chapman (I have forgotten which) had been wounded, and a few other Mosby's men, but none killed. The Yankees had retired to their boats, but had not yet gone away.

The poor wounded horse groaned now and then as we stood by watching it in the soft, spring night with the frogs singing around us. Then Phil and Uncle Charles came and led the horse into a point of woods in the meadow field.

In the morning, soon after breakfast, our own soldiers rode back. The Yankees had been driven back and had gone away. None of our Boys had been hurt, but they had ridden hard, and the day was very warm, especially for March. They were resting and cooling off in the hall with both doors wide open when Mr. Cole rode up. He was the most down-and-out-looking man you ever saw. He had lost his way, had ridden up hill and down, and had not reached Kinsale till after the soldiers had left.

What a shout the soldiers raised! Poor Mr. Cole was a lather of perspiration. The bag of food Mamma had given him was so trounced about that it was one big ball—ham sandwiches, biscuit, eggs—all beaten together till you could hardly tell which was which. Such was the battle of Kinsale. You won't find it in history, children, but it was exciting to us.

—————————————

March passed and April came. We heard a rumor that General Lee had evacuated Richmond, but some of us refused to believe it. There was no singing that night. The soldiers sat around, silent and thoughtful. No one even had the heart to discuss the rumor. The next morning we heard Mad Sally snorting and blowing, and soon saw Cousin Norman riding down the road. Yes, he told us, it was true. Richmond had been given up. He told his news manfully, but I never saw a sadder face. All his bright color was gone. He was ashy pale and complained of a dreadful pain in his head. He told us of the evacuation: how in places the city had been set afire and the streets ran with the whiskey and liquors that were emptied into them.

Only a few days later, all of the soldiers were ordered away. We stood at the door to watch them go. Even the horses moved in a dispirited way. Nobody looked back, only kind Alec Carey rode back to give some thoughtful word of advice "in case Harry has to come."

In case Harry has to come! The thought cut like a knife into our hearts. Harry was barely fifteen.

The next day we heard of the surrender. Poor Mamma went to bed and stayed there. All she had lost had been in vain. In a short while the soldiers of Lee's army came straggling home, one by one. We heard how James Pegrim, an artillery officer, a fine young fellow admired by everyone, when drawn up with his command awaiting the surrender lost his head and opened fire on the enemy's lines. He was so evidently beside himself that the officers of the other side generously tried to spare him, but it was no use. He had to be killed. I have heard he was the last man shot down in the army.

Then came the assassination of President Lincoln. I remember everyone talking about it, and reading the papers when any were to be had, and my Father saying, "In him the South has lost her best friend in the North."

Something strange happened almost every day. The servants went on in their usual ways, but a short while after the surrender, Father called them all into the hall and told them they knew that now they were free people. He told them how much they had been to their white people, and that we loved them and would gladly start them off with some means of livelihood, "but," he said, "we are all poor together." Then he told them if they cared to stay and work the land there might be a division of the crops between him and them. He had no money to pay hire. He told them to think the situation over and let him know what they wanted to do.

The Negroes were very quiet and very respectful. As they went out, they passed my Father and he shook hands with each one.

Uncle Charles already knew what he wanted to do. He said he wanted to go on working his garden the rest of his life and to work for "Miss Mary," but he thought that if he lived off the place he would feel more like a free man. He went immediately to work, and in a few months found a cabin on the road to Warsaw, left his dear little home on the Spring Hill, and went away to live, though he always worked for us. Aunt Eve, his wife, strove her best to keep him from going, but it was to no avail. "Charles is plumb crazy. I wants my own cabin," she complained bitterly. "I don't want to go no whar else."

But Uncles Charles was inexorable. They moved off together.

Phil was the next one to go. We had always depended on Phil—thought of him almost as the foreman on the place. My Father and Mother were disappointed when, without saying anything of his plans, he simply did not appear one morning, and later we learned he had taken work some distance away.

Quite a large force of the Northern army had moved down to Warsaw and had "taken possession" of us. A great many things were occurring that we were too young to understand or appreciate, but it excited us and made us angry to see the Yankees walking about and taking possession. Probably it would have made us feel more so if the officer in command in Warsaw, Colonel Hamilton, had not been the fine man he was. He was as just as he possibly could be—and as considerate—that was what all of our men said of him.

Our men were overwrought because Colonel Hamilton was a Yankee.

Henry T. Ward ("Harry")
in his cadet uniform at the
Virginia Military Institute.

They left him entirely alone, but they appreciated his goodness. The women were worse than the men. I remember passing through the churchyard where neighbor and friend always stopped to speak to each other and have a little chat before going into church. There I always saw Colonel Hamilton standing apart, never in uniform, but always dressed faultlessly for church. I was told never to look at him, but stealthily I always did, and today his face and bearing are clearly before me—deep thought expressed by both. He did not stay with us long as, indeed, we did not deserve to have him. He asked to be relieved of his command because, he said, he could not live where even the children turned from him with horror. I am glad to remember that the evening before he left us, a delegation of the principal men of our community went to see him and in the name of the whole thanked him for his courtesy and consideration.

―⸱⧓⸱―

It was strange to look at Jack and Lewis, Amy and Maria, and know they were no longer our little maids and men. Oddly enough, it seemed to feel very strange to the little blacks themselves. They had been at home with us. Looking back, I cannot remember one word in which any of us were taunted with their being free, either from the grown colored people or from the children. This seems strange to me under the circumstances. We played together as of old and the little darkies did their several jobs.

One very warm July morning, Mamma came down to breakfast to find a plate of badly burned biscuit on the table.

"Jack," she said, "throw those biscuits into the pig pen. They are not fit for the table."

Jack did as he was told, and Silvie was furious. She gathered up all of her children and "went to the Yankees." We found later she had been drinking. Silvie's children were afraid of her when she was in her tempers. Bladensfield had always been their home and our Mother had been their law. They did not want to go with their mother, but of course they had to go.

Colonel Hamilton had gone. There was a Captain Ayres in command at the time. There was nothing he could do for Silvie but advise her to put out herself and her children for hire, which she did, for less money, perhaps, than Papa was paying her. A friend of ours whose servants had left and who knew what a good cook Silvie was hired her, and let her bring her three youngest children with her. The others were hired around among the neighbors. They used to come back to see us when they could. One day, our Father drove to Warsaw and stayed there for several hours. When he reached home and started to unhitch the horse, he found Silvie's little Walter curled up in the buggy box. The child explained that he saw the horse standing there and he wanted to come home. Ran was delighted to see him.

By the fall, all the servants had left except Louisa and her little son. She didn't want to go, but Papa said she was a valuable servant who could command far higher wages in town than he could afford to pay. He insisted upon her going. Finally she agreed. We helped her make her preparations to leave and bade her a loving farewell.

The War was over! We stood facing new and difficult conditions. Father had one silver quarter and a heap of Confederate money, now not worth a dime. He had never ploughed a day in his life, and was no longer young. For a time we thought we should not be able to keep Bladensfield, but it was secured to us. Dear old place, with its dormer windows looking at us through the trees as they had always done; it was still to be our home. What love and protection it expressed, and expresses to us still! Above us arched the blue sky. To us it was a symbol of God's love and care, and that belief was a well of living water to us. We drank of it unquestioningly and drew strength we could have gotten in no other way. I remember that time as a difficult time of change, but shot through with great neighborly good feeling and cooperation and an intense love for our dear South. I remember hearty laughs at awkward attempts to do unaccustomed things. I remember life bravely and cheerfully lived. We were young. We laughed and hoped, loved each other, and did what we could.

Homegoing

Peter Matthiessen

*In memory of E. C. M.,
with love*

Twenty years ago, in April, I first came here to Bladensfield, which lies far out on the Northern Neck of tidewater Virginia, between the Potomac and the Rappahannock Rivers. That winter—it was 1956—my mother had given me a faded typescript of a family document, *The Children of Bladensfield During the Civil War,* a vivid and moving account of an extraordinary period as seen through the eyes of an alert and discerning child. The author, my mother's great-aunt Evelyn Ward, had dedicated her story to "the grandchildren and the great-great-grandchildren of the old place," and as this indiscriminate aggregation happened to include myself, the story filled me with the nostalgia of lost roots; it was not only that Bladensfield was an old place, it was *our* old place, it was still very much in the family, and it seemed important to go there as soon as possible.

As a child of Bladensfield, I knew, I was starting rather late; in 1956, I was already twenty-eight. But Bladensfield is far away from everything, and my mother said, a little sadly, that she had not gone there often, although she had fond memories of the "old place." At the time of her first visit, as a child of ten, just before World War I, five of the twelve children of Bladensfield were already gone, including Will and Charley Ward, whose deaths as brave young soldiers in the Civil War are described so poignantly in the account. Mary Ward Burr was alive, though my mother does not recall her, and so was my great-grandmother, Martha Ward Carey ("Sister Matty"), and the five youngest—Lucy, Evie, and Fonnie; Channing ("Chan") and Randolph ("Baby Ran"). Channing, who died in 1945, was the last of the children of Bladensfield, and it is Randolph's children, William Ward and Cornelia Ward Aldridge, whose families have been living there in recent years.

Of these Bladensfield cousins, the only one I had ever met was Katharine Aldridge, who was discovered by the Powers model agency in 1936 while working as a secretary in Baltimore, and traveled to New York on the condition that her "Cousin Betty"—Elizabeth Carey Matthiessen, my mother—act as chaperone. (My father, with his dread of cousins, was so agreeably surprised by the appearance of Katharine and her sister Clelia that, by his own account, he nearly fell over backward.) As a model, Katharine was destined to become the only person or object ever to appear three times on the cover of *Life* magazine (Winston Churchill made it four times and the Statue of Liberty twice). No doubt she was part of the romantic expectations that filled my heart on that cool, fresh April day in 1956 when I drove eastward down the Northern Neck and—because in those days the old place was still innocent of telephone (and heat and plumbing)—descended upon Bladensfield without warning.

The house lies more than a half-mile south of the Kinsale Road, at the end of a drive—now a shady lane—close-bordered by dogwood, holly, poplars, and one mighty oak, which separate the drive from fields of wheat, corn, and soybean to the east and cool, deep forest to the west. Withdrawing from the outside world, this sand lane passes through a pole gate and an old split-rail fence and subsides into what once had been a formal carriage circle, shaded by great elms.

In forest light, the house rose like a woody growth, dark silver-green with years of weather. Unreasonably, I had expected a white house, but either the paint had worn away or the house had never known a coat of paint at all. The dank green fungus and the rotting weatherboards under the eaves and the broken attic panes deepened its gothic atmosphere; high dormers, narrow gables, bleak uncurtained windows, and a brick foundation rising two feet out of the ground made the house seem higher, gaunter than it was. Its several doors, served by wood steps, looked irrevocably shut, as if its occupants were long gone or had boarded themselves up to close away the modern world at the distant highway.

Two English box trees by this drive, grown gigantesque, stood watch over the house with that air of melancholy wistfulness that is peculiar to formality untended. There was no sign of life, no sound, and instinct forbade me to call out; my presence was already an intrusion. Then the silence was scattered by small-arms fire from an attic window.

In 1956, the only full-time resident of Bladensfield was William Randolph Ward, then sixty-seven, who was doing his best to keep the place from falling into ruin; I wondered if he took me for a Yankee. But soon he came down to the door, explaining even as we introduced ourselves that he was skirmishing with the local woodpeckers, who had been making much too free with the old weatherboarding. What was worse, beavers were ruining the fish pond he had constructed by damming the stream below the house; he was plagued by beavers. Surely not, I said: according to a work on vanishing wildlife in the process of being written by myself, there had been no beavers in Virginia since the eighteenth century. Uncle William, a tall vigorous man with a military mustache, marched me straight down to the pond for a look at his beaver-gnawed stumps, after which, with an improved attitude, I was shown about Bladensfield Plantation.

Uncle William gazed about him at spring woods of beech and hickory, sweet gum and locust, hardhack and foxtail pine. "If we could only have a real story of the people living here from the beginning to the Wards' time, it would be quite interesting," he said. "A lot of Bladensfield's history before the Carters' and Pecks' time is unknown, including the facts about the building of it. We don't even know how it came to the Carters, who owned most of the Northern Neck in those days."

An entry in Robert Carter's daybook for October 27, 1773, shows delivery of corn and wheat from "Billingsgate," but by 1790, when the house was deeded to his daughter, it was already called Bladensfield, after the family of Carter's mother-in-law, the sister of that Thomas Bladen who had been governor of Maryland from 1742 to 1747. The Peck family sold the place to the Reverend William Ward in 1842.

According to a history of the period (*Virginia Cousins*), my great-great-grandfather Ward "was appointed to the U.S. Military Academy at West Point, at the age of twenty, and was a class-mate of General Robert E. Lee, with whom, as well as with Jefferson Davis, who was in the class above him, he kept up a lifelong friendship." Later, however, Ward turned to the ministry, and became rector of three country churches, two of which—North Farnham Parish Church and Yeocomico (built in 1706)—are among the few colonial churches that still stand. It was in this period that he acquired Bladensfield. About 1854 he gave up the ministry under confused circumstances. One day in church a pretty and flirtatious guest of the Tayloes of Mt. Aery so paralyzed him with her fan that he simply fell silent, then forsook the pulpit; old Mr. John Tayloe was outraged that a "family man"—for the Reverend Ward already had many children—should be discomfited so publicly, and persuaded my forebear to resign. Having done so, he turned his full attention to the Bladensfield Female Seminary, a private school he had started in his house in the 1840s, which offered painting and music as well as conventional studies, and was highly thought of in the Northern Neck.

In these years war must have seemed remote, to judge from a letter sent to Ward in 1853 by John Augustine Washington (the last of that family to live at Mt. Vernon) in regard to the hiring of a governess:

Mount Vernon   Oct. 26th. 1853

Rev. W. N. Ward

Dr. Sir

I see yours of the 24th to day recommending Miss Mary Noble to me as a Governess for my children . . . I presume that Miss N. is sound (according to Southern Views) on the subject of Slavery. This is indispensable, as I would not on any consideration, have the views of "Higher Law Abolitionists" instilled into the minds of my Children. I am Sir most respectfully yours

John A. Washington

But this letter was soon to be sadly out of date. A few years later my great-grandmother, already in her twenties, could recall listening in bed one night as her father clumped up and down the hall with General Lee, worrying at the possibilities of war (Lee's birthplace at Stratford Hall was fourteen miles away). Or so, at least, she told my mother, who passed this story on to me. And it is in this uneasy period before the War, just as Lincoln is elected President, that Aunt Evie's account begins, in September 1860. It is autumn again when her book ends, just four years later: how much joy and pain is distilled in those few years!

Now it was 1956, and the house had gone unchanged for ninety years. So far from the highway, in the April sunshine and the light of flowers, the atmosphere of time suspended was uncanny—the children of Bladensfield might come running from the spring at any moment.

Perhaps, had they come, they would have been saddened by the decrepitude of their old house. Yet the interior, as Uncle William said—"all but the attic"—was in good repair, and its rooms, though small in the style of early times, had big windows and were generally light and airy. On the ground floor, four main rooms led into a hall that, crossing the house from north to south, was floored by magnificent pine timbers, thirty-two feet long; this arrangement was repeated on the second floor, where the bedrooms were located. There were also rooms over the kitchen wing, at the east end, which was built in 1847, to house schoolrooms for the Seminary; high dormers for the attic dormitories were built at the same time.

Uncle William showed me a child's highchair, the heavy rungs of which, trod by generations of small feet, his own included, were all but gone. Everywhere door sills were worn down as low as the level of the floor, and even the solid brass of the old doorknobs had rubbed away, so that the knobs looked skinny in their fittings. The rooms were cluttered with antiques and memorabilia, including the Reverend Ward's great Bible, given him by his mother; a chair in which he composed his sermons, Confederate bonds and treasury drafts, an old Currier & Ives, a prototypic kerosene lamp, bought in 1860; spinning wheels, medicine mortars, and works of art by various females of the family, notably my great-grandmother, who had been an admirer of Titian, to judge from a dramatic work hanging among the family portraits in the parlor. There were also three venerable pianos. "This one was bought in 1849," said Uncle William, seating himself and playing me a sprightly song of his own composition.

How incongruous it seemed that my Ward kinfolk, so poor in terms of ready cash, might have solved all immediate problems by selling off a small part of the antiques that filled the house, not to speak of the eight hundred acres of good land that make up Bladensfield and the Porter's Farm of Aunt Evie's account. But apparently this idea was unacceptable, since the antiques were not antiques at all, but things in use, and Porter's was no more separable from Bladensfield

than the wild lawns and overgrown gardens that led down to the old Peck Burying Ground.

Porter's Farm was originally the Cary Tract, after a London merchant of that
name who apparently owned it prior to the Carters; a man named Porter had
acquired it in 1852, and sold it again in the 1870s to my great-grandmother,
Aunt Evie's sister Martha Ward, who was then casting about for a means
of supporting the family. She acquired Porter's not with money, since she had
none, but by selling off the virgin timber on this property, then paying for
the land with the proceeds from the sale of the timber. Martha Ward was enter-
prising and indomitable, qualities that turned a little in her later life and made
her the "livin' terror" of the family. As Uncle William says, "Matty liked to cause
a row wherever she went." Apparently her intransigence commenced at birth, for
when denied anything at all she would terrify her mother by holding her breath
until she became unconscious. Even in Aunt Evie's account, young Sister Matty is invariably forceful, shaming the Yankee lieutenant who took young
Charley prisoner into giving his own coat to the sick boy. After the War, she
turned her painting to good use, selling printed copies of a small oil she had
made of Stratford Hall. The painting was later reproduced in a book of Lee's
memoirs, which noted,

> General Lee's recollections of his childhood home were always as vivid
> as they were tender and pleasant. To the young lady who made the
> sketch of his birthplace, which we give, he wrote the following char-
> acteristic letter:

> Lexington, Va., May 28, 1866

> Miss Matty Ward, Care of Rev. Wm. N. Ward, Warsaw Post Office,
> Va.

> My dear Miss Ward:

> I have just received from Richmond the two photographic copies of
> your painting of Stratford. Your picture vividly recalls scenes of my
> earliest recollections and happiest days. Though unseen for years,
> every feature of the house is familiar to me.

> I return my sincere thanks for the pleasure you have given me, and
> beg you to accept my earnest wishes for your future happiness.

> Your obedient servant,
> R. E. LEE

As the oldest child, Matty intended to see to it that her brother Henry got an education: "If I can only make enough by my picture to send Harry to school," she wrote in March 1866 to her friend Alice Brockenbrough, "I will be a proud and happy woman." To judge from this letter, Matty was at this time the energetic leader of the family. Of her father, *Virginia Cousins* says, "after the death of two sons, a brother, and many relations near to him and dear, who were killed in battle, he became very much changed. 'He was throughout the remainder of his life,' writes a relative, 'like one who walked in a dream; his mind was strong and vigorous when any occasion roused him up.' Ordinarily, however, he looked as if he were living in the faraway past . . ." The Reverend Ward had arranged for Charley's release in a prisoner-of-war exchange, and Charley returned to his company, only to be killed a few months later; then, just after the war, the family lost beautiful Estelle, who died at age fifteen. The Reverend Ward did mission work and directed schools as far from home as Georgia and South Carolina; he died at Bladensfield in 1881.

During the war, young Martha Ward had enraptured my great-grandfather, James Carey, "a Baltimorean exquisite in manners and appearance," as Aunt Evie describes him. Carey had been jailed for having resisted the passage of Butler's troops through Baltimore; once released, he made his way through the lines and took part in the first battle of Bull Run. He was made a captain and an aide to General Hood, but became disgusted with Hood's "unprincipled career," and was trying to join Mosby's Partisan Rangers (Mosby's Raiders) when the War ended. James Carey's younger brother Alec was one of Mosby's men, quartered at Bladensfield, and that is how James Carey came there. He married Matty in 1869 and died in 1877, leaving her penniless.

Like many Southerners, the Wards have faith in the unusual beauty of their women, from "the famous belle Maria Ward" (who married into the Randolphs of Virginia in the early nineteenth century) to Cousin Betty and Cousin Katharine, but possibly young Martha Ward was the most beautiful of all: "The Good Lord," she used to say, turning her head this way and that, "blessed me with this gloe-rious hay-uh."

After her husband died, life was indeed hard for the young widow, who struggled to support herself and her two children by taking student boarders from Johns Hopkins into her house in Baltimore. Many of these youths fell in love with her, so it is said, among them Frederick Warren, who eventually married her daughter, Estelle. Warren later became a professor of French at Yale University (inspiring his wife to a lifelong affectation; as children, we were told to call her "Tante Estelle"). Years later, the Warrens were visited by Matty, who was fond of sitting in an adjoining room while the professor entertained his guests, saying loudly and repeatedly, "Damn Yankees! I can *smell* 'em!"

Meanwhile, Mamie had married DeVere Burr, and Eddie had married Dr. Pearson Chapman (though Edmonia would die in "young middle age," in 1882).

The younger brothers Chan and Ran both became engineers; Randolph Ward built railroads in Cuba, Panama, the Yucatan, and as far away as the Argentine. But no Ward has had much talent for accumulation, and DeVere Burr, a Catholic, was disinherited when Mary Ward insisted on her Protestantism, and after 1881, when their father died, the younger sisters—Lucy, Evie, and Fonnie—moved with their mother to Washington, D.C., where Mary Burr was living. Lucy took a lifelong job at the United States Patent Office, and Evie and Fonnie started a school, The Misses Ward, at 1713 Q Street, where, in the chronic absence of the father, they raised Randolph's young children. None of the three sisters ever married, though Evie especially was very pretty and had lots of suitors, my mother recalls; she blames Aunt Evie's maiden state on the envy of Aunt Fonnie, who was disliked as widely as Evie was adored.

In the 1880s, Henry Ward, the oldest surviving son, was left alone at Bladensfield, and did his best to farm it for the family, but after some years he abandoned it to tenant farmers, and took a position as manager of the Bonaparte estates in Maryland. As the family home, the old place was now empty, but

The painting of General Lee's birthplace by Matty Ward
(P.M.'s great-grandmother).

Cousin Katharine Aldridge at Bladensfield.

all three of the maiden aunts returned each summer, and in 1920 they retired permanently to Bladensfield, where Aunt Evie set down the fresh, amazing memories that make up her book. That same year they were joined by Randolph's children, William Ward and Cornelia Aldridge, recently a widow, whose five children would all be raised at Bladensfield.

In her clear memory and fresh manner of expression, my Cousin Katharine is a worthy heir to her great aunt, and hereafter I shall quote freely from her letters:

> As you can imagine, it was not pleasing to Uncle William's father, Randolph Goode Ward, that sometimes successful promoter-engineer, to have his handsome, well-educated, and world-travelled son retreat to Bladensfield and "bury himself in the woods." Grandpa himself had married a Yankee and gotten out of there at a very early age and thought entirely in terms of The Big World. He lived the universal family dream—I had it, too—of making a fortune and coming home in triumph to restore Bladensfield, but reality turned out very differently. At times he *did* make it, so Mother and Uncle were subjected to extremes of affluence and disappointment, depending on what their absentee father could provide. In my own childhood, I can remember

the mysterious disappearance of this or that piece of jewelry or silver that had been gifts of my grandfather to Mother during one of his hey-day periods. She would reluctantly admit that "Dear Poppa" is having a difficult time getting a deal together in New York City and needs a little money to tide him over but will make it all up to us soon. Your grandfather, my Cousin George Carey, was always very concerned about him and did what he could to help, but as you are aware, his own situation was not too secure. In the end it was Cousin George who got the word through to us, in 1931, that Grandpa was on his uppers in a little room practically in the attic of the old Herald Square Hotel and that he was very ill. So Mary Ward Burr's daughter "Cousin Midge" was dispatched to New York City on the very sad mission of bringing this too proud, glorious old gentleman home to die. Is there anything more poignantly heartrending than the gallant covering-up of financial problems that proud men usually manage?

When they returned to Bladensfield, all three of the great aunts were over seventy, and during Katharine's childhood, the income at Bladensfield was con-fined to small pensions and insurance payments, and such incidental help as the "marvelous boxes of hand-me-downs" that were sent there by my mother.

Many of Cousin Betty's maternity outfits ended up as my regular clothing. Once when Aunt Fonnie heard me inquire why these dresses had such peculiar extendable waistlines, this expression of what she termed "lewd curiosity" convinced her anew that I was a "lascivious and licentious child with a definitely common streak." She was wont to walk around the dining table and on general principles stop at my chair to give me a thump on the head . . . just in case. Once she detected that I had rouged my cheeks and, therefore, pro-ceeded to "box my jaws." To this day I avoid any sort of physical fight encounter but that morning I gave Aunt Fonnie a now-famous uppercut. Incidentally, the source of my rouge was the tiny first-born oak leaves that are such a delicious shade of red. Aunt Evie had told me about this trick of the belles of her day. She also told me that her Mama used to use pokeberries crushed juicy and placed in a hollowed-out pumpkin as a source of dye for their homespun clothes during the Civil War. Another idea I enjoyed was that of wrapping a coiled switch of hair around a rag and then (after covering it for protection) burying it in a pan of dough and cooking it a while so that the moist heat would produce one of those beau-catching neck curls that girls used to attach to their chignons. I was always frantic to have curly hair, and went so far as to eat out of the garbage bucket in the hope of getting typhoid fever and having my straight hair fall out entirely and a new crop come in curling. Aunt Evie said that this had happened to someone she knew after typhoid fever, and so I had high hopes.

It always strikes Sister and me that our Mother and Aunts, and a very few other of their era's Virginia "gentlewomen," personified the profoundest meaning of that word. They were totally incapable of coarseness of any description. Isn't it amazing that in that old house back in the woods and without money, plumbing, heat, radio or phone, the Aunts and Mother somehow conveyed a sense of confidence in the unassailability of our social position. There was never any posturing or affectation in their attitude, just a consciousness of not dropping standards; that we children must not ever behave in such a way that we would be a disappointment to our ancestors or hurt those who were nurturing us. In my own case, modelling had its common aspects, so did Hollywood, and certainly getting myself extricated from my first marriage was a sordid experience, but somehow through it all I have felt at the core uncontaminated because of what I was given by my Mother, the Aunts, and the total ambiance of Bladensfield.

In their memories of the Aunts, I notice, neither Cousin Katharine nor my mother have much to say about Aunt Lucy. Even as a young girl in Aunt Evie's story, Lucy Ward was always helpful and self-effacing, and apparently she retained these qualities throughout her life, which came to an end at Bladensfield in 1932. Randolph Ward had died there in the previous year and Fonnie the year after. William Ward, now in his forties, married and departed, and when Aunt Evie died in 1941, Cornelia Aldridge moved to Katharine's house in California. Although well looked after by black tenant farmers, Bladensfield stood empty once again.

In 1950, Uncle William returned to Bladensfield, this time for good. In 1956, at the time of my first visit, he was all alone there, although his wife and sister and the children of both families joined him whenever they could. Since he regarded it as the homestead, Uncle William was saddened by what he considers a family tendency to drift away, but he was aware that Bladensfield's lack of telephone, heat, and plumbing (an ingenious cold-water system of his own invention did not include a toilet) might dismay less hardy admirers than himself; on the other hand, his age and means set limits on his restorations, and all had to defer to such immediate concerns as new weatherboards and shingles, and a coat of paint: the poplar weatherboards beneath the eaves, said Uncle William, with as much pride as regret, had not been replaced in the two centuries or more since the house was built. He intended to do much of the work himself, for he is an hydraulic engineer and inspired inventor, even if most of the inventions remain in the experimental stage. ("On my first visit," my father recalls, "William was trying to rig an airplane propeller to his outboard, to turn his boat into an autogyro.") On a tour of the attic, I inquired as to the purpose of a wonderful device built into a sturdy Quaker Oats carton, and William nodded his head enigmatically. "This thing has puzzled the engineers for years," he said, turning it over in his big hands, then replacing it without explaining what it was. He gave me a certain look he has—ironic, self-deprecating, wistful. "They couldn't figure it out," he said, "and couldn't duplicate it."

Not long after my first visit to Bladensfield, I had a letter from Uncle William, accepting this northern cousin into a southern family:

> I want to say how pleased I am to know you and I only wish you could have stayed longer so as to know Bladensfield and one of its antiques (me) better. I realize how this house strikes others used to modern, immaculate homes, but it does not pretend to be modern in any way and could not be even with modern facilities. As I told you, it would be wrong to replace worn door sills etc. for the sign of antiquity would thus be removed (yes, strengthen underneath where this will not show). Being past heir to this enormous restoration problem puts me on a spot. I am doing what I can within my means and labor. Yesterday I had a big road machine to widen the drive in from the main road. Tons of honeysuckle, roots, stumps etc. were pushed into gullies and piles before the real road work could begin . . .
>
> Before the Wards' time, there was a much larger pond here, built by John Peck, and it had a grist mill run by water power. Part of the dam is still there, and the road. Some day I have in mind to restore it . . .

He also said that he was installing new poplar weatherboarding and had a plan to paint the house; there was another plan to put in a bathroom with hot water, and a telephone was on its way.

> I think it would do you good to come down again soon. May and June are pretty months here. Lots of flowers in May, and the fish start biting then. I think this place is what many dream of having, so though we are not rich in money matters, we are quite wealthy in other ways.

But it was ten years, perhaps twelve, before I returned to Bladensfield, and that day—a soft copper day of Indian summer—I got no farther than the outer drive. It was a Sunday, I remember, and because of the clearing that had taken place down the straight lane between the trees, I was able to see beyond the inner gate the Sunday colors of the friends who had come that day to visit. The

figures seemed very far away, moving gently among the trees in the autumn silence, as in a fete of the century before.

Not having announced myself, and knowing that these kind cousins would
make too much of me, I backed down the lane in my hired car and went my way
along the concrete road.

Another decade had passed when in November of 1975 I was invited to speak
at the University of Virginia, where Brother Will had completed his education
before going off to war. (On Will's old report card, shown me subsequently by
Cousin Evelyn, I noticed that the teacher in Moral Philosophy was Professor
McGuffey, who brought out *McGuffey's Reader*.) On a bright autumn Saturday,
I drove over from Charlottesville with friends, having first called Katharine (now
living in Maine) to see if anyone was there. "Oh, Uncle's there," said Katharine,
"and Evelyn, too—they'll be so glad to see you!" I asked how Uncle William
was, and she said he was fine. "Eighty-seven, y'know, and still buildin' his wind
machines in the back yard!" Katharine laughed with that affectionate malice that
seems to be a family trait—my mother has it, too. Uncle William is perfectly
aware that the family takes an irreverent view of his inventions, which are all
lumped under the generic term of "wind machines." During this visit, my friends
and I were taken out to inspect the latest, a well-made arrangement of turbojet
compressors and kerosene motor mounted on a small platform set upon four
bicycle tires. On theory, at least, this device could lift its inventor into the air
and bear him away, as he said himself, "to parts unknown." He gave us a long
look, standing there in the cold November air. "The whole thing cost me eighty-
four dollars and my own time," he said quietly, and tapped his temple. "Isn't it
worth that, to keep the old man from going senile?"

I see Uncle as the personification of what young people today mean
when they say of a man that he is Beautiful, and he has Soul in their
meaning of the word. He was many years ahead of them in returning
to the land, and in "doing his own thing," and it took courage to believe in his ability to make it at Bladensfield. Such a man must have
great inner resources; he has always worked hard on his projects and
has depended only on his own resourcefulness. So sure is he in his
knowledge of the basic principles of electrical and mechanical engineering that he has absolute conviction that his flights of creative
imagination will work. I, for one, am convinced that Uncle is some
kind of unrecognised inventive genius; and engineers and inventors
who have sought Uncle out over his years at Bladensfield have expressed great respect for his capacity to comprehend abstract con-
cepts of mathematics and principles of very advanced engineering.
His optimism comes from his faith in his ability; he *knows* that by

proper application of his theories, his space platform (or whatever) *can* take off and soar over the rooftop of Bladensfield. Therefore, we can not accuse him of foolish fantasy. I wonder if he told you about his relationship with the celebrated inventor John Hayes Hammond, who came to Bladensfield to consult him? Also, did you know that Uncle has papers to prove that he expounded the theory of inertial navigation to the Navy years ahead of the construction of the Nautilus? The Navy paid him no heed. Just think how frustrating it has always been for him not to have the finances or laboratory equipment needed to develop his ideas! Uncle is reaching out desperately to be heard before it is too late.

Uncle is still a boy with all his dreams intact, for he is an unquenchable romantic and optimist and so was Mother, who worked very hard on her writing and painting and for some years taught art at St. Margaret's School in Tappahannock. How *wonderful* it is at any age to retain the expectation of a miracle and to believe in our dreams! Do you know that Mother used to walk to the corner Post Office every day, four miles round trip, in anticipation of hearing that she had won this or that contest, that her book had been accepted, that she had sold a story, poem, or painting? She was thought to have psychic powers, you know, and used to rock contentedly and speak naturally of "your dear father trying to get through to me." Once, at a psychic meeting after Aunt Fonnie had died, the medium told the audience that a spirit was attempting to reach a Cornelia Ward and Annetta Chapman. Cousin Annetta is quoted as having exclaimed: "Oh my God No! We certainly do *not* want any messages from Aunt Fonnie! We heard far too much from her when she was alive." The part that is most difficult to believe is that Aunt Fonnie's ghost, intimidated, departed without a word.

Katharine's mother had died since my first visit, but Uncle William's wife Evelyn had given up her teaching and returned permanently to Bladensfield; their daughter "Young Evie" Milsted, with her three children, was also living there, and so was a cousin called "Bill Burr"—not "Bill," but in the southern usage, plain "Bill Burr." They all came out and lined up on the driveway, as people did when courtesy was still in fashion, from little Edgar Milsted, five years old, to Uncle William, eighty-seven, white-haired now but still erect and very tall. Although she and I had never met, Cousin Evelyn called out warmly, "Hello, Peter! You are all too late for the peanut-butter sandwiches!" Everyone laughed at this joking reference to the family's straitened means. ("Please don't think we're not capable of laughing at ourselves," Evie Milsted would say on a more serious occasion. "Perhaps it's that we've laughed so much that now we ache.")

Bladensfield was the family home again, and I knew right then that my mother must be persuaded to return here for a visit; she had not been here since Aunt Evie's funeral in 1941, and she would certainly be interested in all the changes. The fabled telephone had come, there was a heater in the dining room, and real hot water; there was also a toilet that sat proudly in the very center of the downstairs bathroom, as if inviting admiring visitors to walk around it. But what had changed most was the outside of the house, now painted white; for some reason, the old place looked much smaller.

Cousin Katharine, for one, was not altogether pleased by these improvements.

Sadly you are too late to talk with the three very remarkable women [Aunts Lucy, Evie, and Fonnie] who dominated my mother and Uncle William's lives and then took us on . . . all five father-less Aldridges when 'Poor dear Cornelia' was widowed. It was they who gave the place its fascination for me and I miss terribly their determination that Bladensfield should remain authentic even if shabby and rundown. For instance, the patina that had over the several hundred years given the old clapboard its silvery mossy tones has all been replaced and painted, thus revealing the lack of architectural design of the original house, plus the off-balance addition put on by my great-grandfather —your great-great, I believe. Just as too much make-up in old age reveals and distorts more than it enhances, so it is with renovations. And even the very necessary steps that have been taken to heat the old house and provide plumbing have for me greatly reduced its charm and challenge. In my childhood, all furniture that was common or 'tacky' was relegated to the attic. Everything was very uncomfortable and inconvenient and the gaping holes in the plaster over our beds created in me a lifetime fear of ghosts and darkness . . . I wonder if you have noticed how much Virginia boxwood smells like a cat pan . . . well, Bladensfield was redolent with both sources of this peculiar fragrance, for in my day the whole place was overrun with cats. My older brother John used to provoke the greatest nostalgia for the old place by reminding me how the old cushions on the hall sofas (those converted rifle-box resting places) now used as hard benches, were delightful places to lie and enjoy the summer breezes which brought out the pungent smells of the old cushions. Perhaps the nose remembers best of all.

And so, on our journey to Bladensfield at Easter in 1976, I was fascinated to see what my mother would recall. We drove up from Richmond on a lovely late afternoon of an unseasonable spring day (it was ninety degrees) and Cousin Betty, to give her her Bladensfield name, took the greatest pleasure in the different greens of the southern countryside, the redbud and dogwood and tall foxtail pines. Toward evening, we passed through the village of Tappahannock, on the Rappahannock River, where the Reverend Ward had been principal of the Tappahannock Seminary for Young Ladies, just before the War; the Wards' "Old Grey House," still standing there just a few years ago, has given way to a concrete parking lot. Across the street was the old Court House, scene of the slave auctions described in Aunt Evie's account; and in this street new recruits were drilled by the former schoolmaster, now Major Ward of the Fifty-fifth Virginia Infantry, whose commission had been sent down from Richmond (his daughter tells us) by President Jeff Davis himself. But most of the other scenes of those spirited days—such as the "Long Bridge" where Cousin Philip Lewis (who would also die) made his gallant ride—are long since gone; only the broad brown river of the tidewater remains the same, stretching a mile across to the dark green forests of the Northern Neck where Bladensfield lies hidden.

Across the river, we turned eastward on the winding roads, arriving toward dusk at the unmarked gate of Bladensfield. The day had been exceptionally hot, and my mother, who is seventy-three, was tired, but even in the near-darkness of our arrival, the memories of evening walks on the old road came flooding back, and of the mimosa blossoms, used by the children to powder their noses yellow, and the chinquapin nuts that were gathered in early fall. Soon we were far distant from the road at the inner gate; through the old trees came the soft glow of the house, the light broken by the overgrown box trees, locust, and magnolia, and a gigantic osage orange, with its gnarled trunk, like a tree out of a tale.

In hot weather at Bladensfield the family sits in the main hall, which extends straight across the house from north to south and draws all the cool breezes. There, under Uncle William's approving gaze, Cousin Betty was welcomed home with a glass of bourbon. A gentle evening was spent enjoying the soft air and the fresh narcissi on the table, the old pictures on the walls, and the old stories —how General Lee had walked this floor with Papa, and how these two Confederate rifle crates, now converted to hall benches, were snatched by the Fifty-fifth Virginia Infantry from beneath Mamma's bed at Tappahannock ("No time for modesty now, Ma'am!"), how black Louisa had been fooled into opening this strong south door, admitting those Yankees who took away poor Charley. And then Cousin Betty was shown to the south room on the second floor where "sweet Alice Peck," and later her own great-grandfather had died. Death is at home in this old house—"Fonnie died right there where that piano is," Uncle William had said earlier, down in the dining room. As for myself, I slept in "Papa's bed," a magnificent four-poster of tiger maple in the Bee Room; here Charley had lain on the fateful night that he was captured. The family says that the Bee Room is haunted—footsteps and the creak of the old rocking chair are heard quite often from the attic—and sometimes the magical "snaps" in the thin air that were also heard—indoors and out—in the vicinity of Aunt Evie. For a

The Bee room.

long time, in the swarming heat, surrounded by ancient and mostly ugly wardrobes, washstands, candle lanterns, and clothes chests of an America now almost gone, I listened to a whippoorwill in the locust trees outside; and lying there in the big bed, in my own middle age, I felt secretive, safe, and innocent and exultant, like a little boy.

Next morning I went out at first light and walked around the grounds as the sun rose, pale and misted, from the southern hardwood forest that is still extensive on this far region of the Northern Neck. The warbler migration had not yet begun, but the birds of orchard and wood edge were abundant, and in the stillness, between ringing sunrise songs of titmice, bobwhites, Carolina wren, the sweet, small voice of a field sparrow could be heard from far away. At the east end of the house, red-bellied woodpeckers joined the cardinals on the seed tray, and the new sun glowed in their spring reds; through the window behind the busy birds I saw the gray head of Cousin Evelyn, who smiled at me as she bustled back and forth getting the breakfast.

Cousin Evelyn, who is years younger than Uncle William, is a warm, humorous, energetic woman who knows more about Bladensfield than her husband's family, having taken the trouble to pursue researches that the Wards never got around to; while Uncle William chooses to accept the Rochester tradition that Aunt Evie writes of in her foreword, Evelyn believes that the Rochester house was actually built on the far side of the Kinsale Road, and that Bladensfield was constructed by the Carters, possibly to house the manager of this outlying plantation that was known originally as Billingsgate. As Uncle William says, "Mother will run down the age of this place, and I will run it up." And it was Evelyn who was bothered most by her husband's decision in recent years to sell off the valuable hardwood timber on what was known as Porter's Farm in Aunt Evie's account; in his mind, he had managed to separate this tract from Bladensfield, while Evelyn felt that an integral part of the old place had been desecrated.

In regard to the land, Uncle William has no nostalgia for old times, and approves wholeheartedly of bulldozers, which have made his pond construction so much simpler: "You're looking at a fella who is eighty-seven years old, and as modern as anyone you'd care to meet." Twenty years ago at the time of my first visit, when William supervised the farming, there was a fine smell here of horse and harness, but the horses have departed now, the pigsties rot along the wood edge, and the farm machinery is rusting in the weeds behind a sagging shed; the mineral smell of the forest has returned. One hundred and twenty-five acres are still planted, mostly in wheat and corn (the same crops were planted in the eighteenth century, when this was Billingsgate), but the fields are leased, and are worked in a matter of hours by huge combines. "I've been retired," Uncle William says approvingly, "like the one-horse farmer."

After breakfast, Uncle William led me on a walk through Timbers Farm, as he calls Porter's, driving around to the south side of the tract, then walking a cool road through second-growth woods to a broad field nearly one half mile across that is leased to a farmer who grows wheat; beyond the woods on the far side of the field lies Peck's Pond, which roughly separates Timbers Farm from Bladensfield. "Take you all day to walk this property," Uncle William said with satisfaction, waving his hand to shoo away the distant racket of a chain saw as he might have waved at the halo of midges that now circled his felt hat. "That childish fella over there . . ." he said, but left this thought unfinished. The day was already very hot, and in the shadow of the wood edge, we stood in silence for a while, listening to the *ky-reer* of a red-tailed hawk, making strong circles high over the fields.

Uncle William turned suddenly and smiled at me, as if sharing a secret. Content, in silence, we returned slowly through the hot, coarse woods, so different from the high forest on the north part of the farm that belonged to another time. At the wood edge we were met by Cousin Betty and Young Evie, who took us on a visit to Sabine Hall, not far from Bladensfield.

Sabine Hall became the Carter homestead when Nomini Hall burned down on Christmas Day of 1850, and Dabney Wellford, a descendent of Landon Carter, was kind enough to show us this fine house, which is constructed around a broad central hall that runs from the carriage circle in the north to the gardens in the south. Bladensfield has the same arrangement, but everything about

"Deepwood."

Sabine Hall is on a grander scale, of finer quality and better kept in all respects —so much so that Cousin Betty, an accomplished horticulturist, commented with vague regret on Bladensfield's lost gardens. Yet the maintained air of Sabine Hall and the broad prospect that stretches away over open country toward the distant glint of the Rappahannock deprives this lovely place of the romantic mystery of Bladensfield, hidden away in its old forest, far from roads.

There is a story written by Aunt Evie called "The Ghosts of Deepwood" which begins as follows:

> Down in Virginia, there is an old place—Deepwood, I will call it— where the sunshine is different from that of any other place on earth; the flowers overrun their world, and bloom more; the birds sing sweeter songs. Why, no one knows; but everyone knows that this is true—at least, everyone who has lived there, and who has a better right to know than they?
>
> The place is deep down in the woods, and very old. . . .

Even with white paint, Bladensfield retains the air of "Deepwood," and John Dos Passos, who came here as a neighbor and friend of Uncle William, was apparently enchanted by the place. So was Cornelia Aldridge's guest, the historical novelist Frances Parkinson Keyes, who used it as the basis of a work called *Fielding's Folly*. I, too, am enchanted, and returning to Bladensfield, I had an undeserved sense of going home. "It was lovely to see the dear woods again," Aunt Evie says, "to drive under the big oaks, all of them misty with the promise of spring. . . ." Some of those big oaks are gone, but the spring promise lingers.

While Cousin Betty helped Evelyn prepare some lunch, Uncle William got me into his '56 Chevy and drove me down to the Seven Acres Pond where he had showed me beaver stumps twenty years before. From a wood bench on the shady dam, we watched a blue-winged teal come tipping in through the high forest and climb out again, while Uncle William discoursed on the joys of pond construction. In the corner of the pond lay the old boat that had been rigged up as a wind machine ("That damned hovercraft never *did* work," its inventor said, disgusted with it still), and below the dam lay the remains of an old hydraulic generator that had failed to supply electricity to the house. Uncle William sighed. "Bill Burr will go swimming with you," he said. "I guess my swimming days are about over. Swam across the Rappahannock in 1925—took me an hour and a half. There were five of us, and three made it—the other two were picked up on the buoys. All dead now, the whole outfit, all but me. I guess the Devil doesn't want me."

Uncle William gave me that sly look of his that is also slightly sad, as if to say, "I wonder if you *really* know why I am smiling?" We contemplated each other for a little while, and then he said, "I tell you what; if you ever start anything up North that you can't finish, you just come on down here, and I'll take care of it."

With Bill Burr, I went to the old Spring House at the branch in the deep woods, to gather some fresh watercress for lunch; it was from this place that the children of Bladensfield went "tugging up the hill," and perhaps they heard a forebear of this wood thrush, or the soft passing of spring breezes in the hickories. Bill Burr showed me the simple ram device, run by the stream, that has pushed cold water to the topmost floor of Bladensfield since 1920: some of our old relative's inventions are quite masterful. "They almost work," Bill Burr remarked. "That's what people don't realize—they almost work. If he had ever got one finished before somebody else stole his idea, he could have been rich." Like Evie Milsted, Bill Burr has come back to Bladensfield at a time of change in his own life. He is fifty-four, a lifelong bachelor, short-spoken and reserved, who seems to speak gruffly when he speaks at all, but in fact, he is considerate and helpful, and a friend to everyone from young Edgar Milsted to "Uncle," as William Ward is

Aunt Evelyn Ward with the Carey children (left to right: Churchill, Elizabeth [P.M.'s mother], and James) at Bladensfield.

called by almost everyone. I, too, think of him as "Uncle," since I feel so at home when I'm around him. He seems to have taken the place of his first cousin, my dead grandfather, George Carey, whom until now I had not known that I had missed.

That afternoon, I accompanied my mother on a walk under the huge elms (the modern blight called the Dutch elm disease has not reached "Deepwood") and pignut hickories, sweet gum and tall tulip trees that dominate the hardwood forest to the north. We walked to the gate where brave young Charley, riding off to war, was seen for the last time, and afterward, we circled round to the Burying Ground to the south, and looked in vain for old Peck gravestones in the tangle. And watching my mother, I felt a warm surge of contentment, for the worry lines that she had brought here had already left her face. Gazing about, she looked so wide-eyed and so innocent that I could perceive her as she must have looked on this same spot in 1913, at the age of ten. And sure enough, her memories were coming back, one after another.

The Careys had come down for the summer, and the children all got typhoid fever about six weeks after they arrived. Aunt Evie was very nice to the sick cousins, but Aunt Fonnie had been stiff and distant, accusing them of bringing typhoid "from the North"; it wasn't until Fonnie contracted it herself that it was traced to a dairy servant here at Bladensfield, which in those days, Cousin Betty recalled—and she turned in a circle as if in hopes that she might glimpse them—had several barns and haylofts, now all gone.

During that stay, the great-uncles came to visit. One night when she could not sleep, either Uncle Chan or Uncle Ran came up and talked to her a little, then tucked the bedclothes very high around her neck, and she fell asleep instantly. (At that time, William was already twenty-four, and just as handsome as he is today.) Why she had thought of this, she did not know. Cousin Betty laughed, remembering how her brother Jim was bitten by a bat while trying to fondle it. Her mother Polly Carey would wear a linen napkin on her head at breakfast, as protection against the bats that roamed the house, and that bat napkin seemed to symbolize a running battle that Polly conducted with her mother-in-law, the formidable Matty, who insisted that the Carey children pronounce Carter "C-yah-tuh" and garden "g-yah-den." Polly once said, "That is not good English," and Matty retorted, "That is the English that is spoken by ladies and gentlemen." (As Katharine has noted, in reference to a relative-by-marriage, "It was ingrained in all Wards, of course, that anyone they married was beneath them in good blood, but this family had excellent brains instead, a very-much-needed gene addition to the Ward line.") Since my grandmother Carey was of the family of Governor Horatio Seymour of New York, she did not regard the Ward blood as one bit better than her own, and refused to bow to the old lady on this point or any other.

"There was something serpentine about my grandmother," Cousin Betty reflected, "a genius for encouraging discontent." And she remembered now how a friend of her mother had once crept out through the children's window to escape this terrible old lady, telling Betty to tell her mother that she—the friend —was fleeing to the beach. When Matty finally gave up on this world, in 1921, Polly Carey said to her young daughter, "You need *not* attend that funeral, and you *may* wear your pink suit." Remembering this, my mother laughed in a peal of real delight.

We were silent for a while in the sun and shadow, and I wondered what my grandfather had made of these mighty women. I was still a child when, after years of drinking and long solitary walks, George Carey waded out into a mill pond with his pockets full of stones, leaving behind the warmest impressions of his gentleness and kindness among all who knew him. I remember best his wonderful and witty stories, with strange heroes such as "Jack the Pig." And now, returning through the twilight to the house, my mother reminisced in a thoughtful way about her father, what a gay fellow he had been, a dancer and singer who whistled so merrily that he was known to his many friends as "Bird"—an idealist of impossible integrity, she said, entirely unsuited to the business world, and also ill-suited to his wife, who was an idealist as irreconcilable as himself. Most of the time the Careys had no more money than the Wards, and my mother had gone to the Ethel Walker School on scholarship.

George Carey
(P.M.'s grandfather).

In the skirmishes with his mother, George Carey had had no choice but to take sides with his wife, and it is for this reason that Porter's Farm passed out of the Carey family, thus changing our whole relationship to Bladensfield. I repeated what Uncle William had told me over there this morning, how Martha Carey had offered that property to her son George, and how my grandfather had refused it as a matter of principle ("That was just like him!" Cousin Betty exclaimed, in mixed love and exasperation), whereupon it was presented to Estelle Warren. But Tante Estelle detested Bladensfield, and her children and grandchildren never came here; her son, James Carey Warren, sold Porter's in 1948 to Uncle William, who renamed it Timbers Farm, after the purpose he had in mind.

One early morning, I went with Cousin Betty on an exploration of the attic, from which nothing seems to have been thrown out since antebellum days. Outside the Long Room (the erstwhile dormitory of the Bladensfield Female Seminary) there is a cobbler's bench with tiny half-made shoes, old cribs and tin baths, hoop skirts and spinning wheels, and even some cloth samples from cotton that was grown, spun, and dyed at Bladensfield during the War. Inside, wood ox yokes and kitchen implements and leather trunks live indiscriminately with

The attic.

paintings, a child's potty chair, school desks and slates, and a variety of "wind-machines," including the small, enigmatic one housed in the Quaker Oats carton —my favorite of twenty years ago.

And my mother was struck, as I had been, by the sheer proliferation of antiques—not "priceless heirlooms" but the plain old things made well at home by the artistic family of a country parson. The huge old "Baby House," built by the servants and mentioned in Aunt Evie's chronicle, still stands in the upstairs hall. Cousin Betty recalled how often she had played there when that summer visit in 1913 extended well into the autumn due to the illness of young Churchill Carey; the Baby House is still occupied by dolls—cherished, battered, many times repaired—who were known to the children of Bladensfield more than a century ago.

That evening I sat up very late, poring over the old books and albums of daguerrotypes and documents and letters that Cousin Evelyn has saved out from the collection of Ward family memorabilia that is now at the Library of Congress: I discovered with pleasure that through my great-great grandmother, I am distant kin to Mark Catesby, the great English naturalist whose work I refer to sometimes in my own. I found old diaries of Aunt Evie, and the first entry is, "My Harry died in Washington, Feb. 10, 1907. . . ." The next is not made until March 5, 1912, when she declares that her diary will be open to any in the family who are interested. Glancing ahead to 1924, I found a letter to the Aunts from Cousin

Betty, with news of her impending marriage to Erard Matthiessen, and for May 22, 1927, there is the following inscription: "Sunday. Betty's son was born. George [my grandfather] wrote that he was to be named Peter . . . June: He is named Peter. He is a dear baby." So far as I know, this is the only record of my arrival, which had been obscured by news of Lindbergh's solo flight over the Atlantic the day before.

At dawn next morning, I walked across the farm from north to south, down past Peck's Pond: as promised in 1956, Uncle William had restored this mill pond from the swamp it had become in the past century, and wild duck—gadwall— rose from black pools at the upper end. Across the mill dam, a path climbed onto Timber Farms, and looking back across Peck's Pond to Bladensfield, I paused in springtime sadness and strange pang of loss.

Later I walked in deep woods with my mother, who rediscovered the pipsis- sewa and the lavender swamp violets, the golden sheen on the sapling leaves of tulip trees, the woodland birds: the Milsteds led us down a stream that would go eventually to the Rappahannock, and Edgar wondered if a sharp rock he had found was made by Indians. Over the night, the warblers had come on spring migration, for an ovenbird was calling from the brown shades, and at the stream edge a pair of water thrushes were teetering and dipping in a delicate dance in the spring light. And my mother was saying, and I nodded, how happy she was that she had come back to Bladensfield, how important it was that Bladensfield stay in the family. Evie Milsted said, "If we didn't have Bladensfield, it doesn't seem to me that life would have so much meaning." Evie looked astonished, as if her own perception had taken her by surprise, and for some reason, I heard an echo of Aunt Evie's voice: ". . . our Charley! Barely eighteen, shot in his own Virginia fields."

If a life of total unselfish service to others is the qualification for saint- hood, then Aunt Evie was a saint. The regular church services she conducted for us each Sunday at Bladensfield carried such conviction that we who were her only parishioners find the faith we have encoun- tered since in ordained churches extremely shallow. Aunt Evie's Christ- mas message was a deeply-felt celebration of the birth of Jesus and the great mystery of His life and message. She approached death as the greatest adventure of all, and when I saw her for the last time, she was happily preparing for her departure, completing journals, labelling family treasures, laying out her funeral clothing in a convenient drawer, and expressing the hope that no foolish doctor would be called in to prolong her life when the moment came to leave it. I recall that she remarked lightly that she had enjoyed her trip years ago to Europe and expected this one to be much more interesting and mysterious. She seemed absolutely certain that she was going to enjoy Heaven

Randolph G. Ward
("Baby Ran") in 1893.

and was passionately impatient to rejoin all her departed loved ones. She patted my sliding straight hair and said gently, "Oh, Katharine, I wish I could leave you the waves in my hair."

The heat of this late April morning brought back to Cousin Betty that day in early May of 1941, when she came down here for Aunt Evie's funeral; "The doors were open," she said, "and there were bees drowsing in and out in the soft light and warm air, and wild flowers everywhere." In the remembrance, she stopped walking, and gazed past me. "Aunt Evie's was the first dead body that I ever saw." I asked how the sight of death had struck her, that first time, and she said it hadn't bothered her. "Aunt Evie looked just fine," said Cousin Betty peacefully, turning away again, and walking on.

I see her now, and I will always see her in those quiet woods, for within the year my mother would be dead—killed untowardly in a violent accident on the public highway. "I like to think," Katharine remarked, "that now in Heaven all the children of Bladensfield are on hand to welcome Cousin Betty—loveliest flower of us all, though I'm sure your Tante Estelle would not admit it."

In early September of this Bicentennial Year, my indomitable Uncle William cracked a vertebra in his back while helping to haul a heavy log from his fish-pond spillway. "I got back from the hospital Sunday," he wrote from Bladens-field on the first day of the fall, "and am glad to be here. I understand from x-rays that a vertebra is shortened some, so am not as tall as I was." However, he is very busy. Recently, he says, "I wrote an article about myself called 'Why?'," and he is currently engaged in exciting correspondence; two big steel companies, under pressure from the Environmental Protection Agency, are studying his method of manufacturing steel with no pollution, which would revolutionize the entire industry. Of the heads of Engineering and Research with whom he is dealing, he remarks, "old-timers do not change, but have to give in to progress." Anxious to get back to work, he signs off, "Best love, Hastily, William."

It is restful to think that the last of the Ward name at Bladensfield will always be there; he has selected the place where he will lie, at the brow of the hill above his beloved pond. As Katharine says, "He wants his feet on the downhill side so that he will be in a position to make sure that 'those damn beavers are not up to any mischief.' It would be unthinkable to carry Uncle off to the Hollywood Cemetery in Richmond—he abominates all cities. For him, Bladensfield *is* Paradise, so who needs to go anywhere?"

*William and Evelyn Ward
at Bladensfield, 1977.*

1. Martha Ward
(1837–1921)
married 1869
James Carey
(1832–1875)

2. William Norvell Ward
killed in Civil War
(1839–1862)

3. Mary Ward (Burr)
(1840–1925)

4. Edmonia Ward (Chapman)
(1842–1882)

5. Charles Blincoe Ward
killed in Civil War
(1845–1863)

6. Lucy Ward
unmarried
(1847–1932)

The Reverend William Norvell Ward
(1807–1881)
married 1836
Mary Blincoe
(1815–1899)

7. Henry Tayloe Ward
(1849–1932)

8. Estelle Ward
unmarried
(1851–1866)

9. Evelyn D. Ward—AUTHOR
unmarried
(1853–1941)

10. Florence Ward
unmarried
(1855–1933)

11. Channing Moore Ward
(1857–1945)

12. Randolph Goode Ward
(1860–1931)
married 1882
Belle Manning Browne
(1861–1945)